CLASSIC THAI FOOD

Delicious Recipes by the Master Chef of Thailand

Srisamorn Kongpun

Translated by
Masiri Anamarn
Amornrat Chareonchai

CLASSIC
THAI FOOD

Delicious Recipes by the Master Chef of Thailand

ASIA
BOOKS

Asia Books Co., Ltd.
Berli Juker House, 99 Sukhumvit 42 (Soi Rubia)
Prakanoang, Klongtoey, Bangkok 10110 THAILAND
www.asiabooks.com

CLASSIC THAI FOOD

9 7 8 9 7 4 8 3 0 3 9 9 4
Printed in Thailand
Distributed by Asia Books Co., Ltd.
Photographs & Design by Samart Sudto

National Library of Thailand Cataloging in Publication Data
Srisamorn Kongpun.
    Classic Thai Food.-- Bangkok : Asia Books, 2013.
    160 p.
    1. Thai food. I. Masiri Anamarn, Amornrat Chareonchai, tr. II. Title.
641.59593

CONTENTS

INTRODUCTION

It is not difficult to cook Thai food nowadays because it is easy to find ingredients such as spices and herbs required to make curry pastes. Ready-made curry pastes and coconut milk can be bought anywhere.

However, a good cook must have an understanding and knowledge of Thai food and culture to be able to select the ingredients to use, because each Thai dish uses a different curry pastes. This book tells you the ingredients of various curry pastes, so you can make your own and keep them frozen to be used over a long time.

Each Thai dish has its own distinctive flavor, aroma and color. If one uses red curry pastes to make *choo chee*, the result will not have the *choo chee* flavor. One needs to have an understanding of different curry pastes ingredients in order to make the correctly flavored, scented, and colored dish.

It is my intention for everyone to be able to use this book to make Thai food quickly while still retaining the same good taste and flavor every time. There is no need to start from scratch each time, which may require a long time.

Recipes in this book differ from those in my previous cookbooks. My original intention was to help restaurant cooks to be able to make each dish quickly. The food will be of good quality and taste, with the same flavor, aroma, and color.

Another purpose of mine is to help those who want to cook their own food to be able to control the use of cooking oil, fish sauce and sugar. Recipes in this book tell you how to prepare ready-made curry bases and salad dressings. This book contains recipes that readers can cook up to standard and then store in a refrigerator. For example, green curry can be made by adding cooked chicken to the heated green curry base, and then adding the eggplants, kaffir lime leaves and sweet basil. This can be done in just 6-7 minutes. The resulting chicken green curry will taste as if it has been newly made. Without being told, no one will be able to tell that the curry base and cooked chicken had been previously prepared.

If the recipes in this cookbook are followed, you will get the same result every time. The flavor, taste, color, and aroma of your dish will be the same as that made by the recipe owner herself. You will see that each Thai dish has a well blended taste. The wonder of Thai dishes lies in this expert blending of tastes.

Ingredients in Thai food not only give a good taste, but also offer good nutritional and medicinal values. Thai food is healthy food. The good taste comes from a well-portioned blend of ingredients in the dish. The food is naturally good. There are no chemicals added to affect aroma, taste or color. I would like to offer those who have never tasted or wanted Thai food to try to follow the recipes in this cookbook. You will have a good Thai dish made with your very own hands.

With Love
Srisamorn Kongpun

THE POPULARITY OF THAI FOOD

Why do foreigners love Thai cuisine so much that Thai cooks are one of the most sought after cooks? Many chefs have changed their careers to learn to be Thai cooks. They hope to become Thai cooks because this is the profession sought after by Thai restaurants in Thailand and abroad.

Answers received from interviewing Thai food lovers are that they love Thai food because they know what they are receiving from Thai food. They know that Thai food is not fattening. After a Thai meal, they can sleep comfortably without indigestion. It is accepted that Thai food is healthy because it contains little cooking oil and a small amount of meat. Each dish contains vegetables or needs to be eaten with vegetables.

Thai food is also popular because each Thai dish has its charm in the well blended and complimentary tastes. The consumers feel the mystery of different tastes in the same dish. When they blend together, the final result is deliciousness. Beyond the good taste, the dishes offer nutritional and medicinal values.

In Thai culture, people eat a set of dishes. Many dishes are served together in a *"sumrub."* The art of eating Thai food is to eat the main dish with complimenting side dishes. For example, when a hot dish is eaten, a bland dish will tone down the heat; similarly, a hot dish will be eaten with rice and followed by a soup such as *tom yum* (spicy and sour soup), or *tom kha* (galangal flavored soup). A *nam prik* (spicy dip) is eaten with vegetables.

Not only is the Thai way of dining delicious, but it also brings a beauty in eating. Each dish contains different kinds of nutrients. Nutrients work together in the body. Various nutrients must be present at the same time for the body to benefit from them.

To be a good Thai cook, one must learn that Thai food is the result of collected knowledge from Thai ancestors. Each Thai dish has its own distinctive characteristics, and has many tastes in one dish. Each taste compliments the other to become delicious. For example, the sourness of lime in *tom yum goong* is reduced by the heat of the bird's eye chili. The heat of the chili is balanced by the shrimp and the shrimp tastes better when the lemongrass is eaten afterwards.

Moreover, Thai food from different regions has different tastes, aromas, colors, and characteristics from ingredients native to the region. The distinctive identity of each regional food may be defined as follows:

Northern Thai Food The taste is not strong. The food is fatty. Sugar is not usually used. Spiciness may be added according to one's preference. For example, fried ground dried chilies may be added to *nam-ngeo* (rice noodle with spicy pork sauce) and *kao soi* (northern-style chicken noodle soup).

Northeastern Thai Food The taste is strong. Most Northeastern food has two basic tastes: salty and hot.

Southern Thai Food The food is hot from the use of many spices and herbs. Turmeric is used in almost every dish.

Central Thai Food Many tastes are properly combined to give a well rounded, tender, mild taste. For example, *pad gaprao* is hotter than *panang*, and *panang* is hotter than *choo chee*. A small amount of sugar is added to each dish to give a tender all around taste.

EATING HEALTHY, EATING THAI

Thai food is considered the best health food because it always contains vegetables or is eaten with vegetables, and consumers receive nutrients from these local or in-season vegetables. Thai food also contains high fiber and low fat. The important thing is that there are no food additives to improve taste, smell or color; sweetness, for instance, comes from coconut milk or sugar. It can be said that Thai food tastes good from a combination of various ingredients without added help.

Some Thai dishes, such as green curry and *tom khaa gai*, were said to contain a high content of fat from coconut milk. This led to a research on Thai food. The finding was that Thai food contains only 20 percent fat on average. Almost all Thai dishes contain vegetables. Even the fat in Thai dishes is eradicated by the inclusion of spices and herbs in curry paste or other contents of each dish such as garlic, shallot, chili, turmeric, galangal, lemongrass, and more. Below are easy ways to use Thai food to relieve or prevent common illnesses:

Knee aches (not gout). Eating food containing ginger can relieve the infection. This includes foods such as stir-fried pork with ginger, *tom som* (tamarind soup), fish soup with ginger and fermented soybeans, ginger chili dips, and *miang kum* (leaf-wrapped appetizer).

Gout. Avoid all kinds of animal innards and eat mostly fish. Use vegetables in food but avoid tender top parts. Take seeds out of vegetables which come from fruit or pod parts. Shoots, seeds and leafy tops will make the aches worse. (For example, remove seeds from cucumbers, avoid the tender top parts of ivygourd, and discard the top part of bean sprouts.) Drink lemongrass tea and drink 8-10 glasses of water each day.

High blood cholesterol. Eat high fiber foods, avoid giblets, sea food, shrimps, shells, crabs, high fat food and animal fat.

High blood pressure. Control the amount of fat, sugar and salt in food. Eat whole grain rice and reduce food containing coconut milk. Use high fiber vegetables in cooking, such as pea eggplants and wild bitter gourd. 200 grams of vegetables should be eaten daily. Use more garlic than usual because garlic can reduce blood pressure.

Insomnia. Always eat whole grain rice. Eat a lot of vegetables and fruit each day (for example, eat a total of 200 grams of all combining vegetables, one orange, one serving of papaya or 8 pieces, and one serving of pineapple or 8 pieces).

Constipation. Make a habit of eating ripe papaya and drinking tamarind juice. Eat whole grain rice, high fiber vegetables such as pea eggplants, which you can boil and then eat with *nam prik* or make egg plant *nam prik*. Wild bitter gourds can be pan-fried with egg. *Sa-dao* can be made into soup with ground pork. Try spicy and sour soup with sesbania flowers, ivygourd leaves and *gaeng liang* (spicy vegetable soup) with banana flower, blanched *sa-dao* eaten with sweet and sour sauce, *gaeng liang* with *cha-om* omelet and grilled fish, and pea eggplant salad. Local vegetables of Thailand that revealed to have medicinal value includes cassia flowers and young leaves *(kee lek)*, which can be cooked with grilled pork in *gaeng pa* (jungle curry, or curry without coconut milk).

Flatulence and indigestion. Eat vegetables which have medicinal value to help digestion, especially of starchy foods. For example, eat ivygourd leaves with *nam prik* or put them in spicy vegetable soup. Try eating pineapple, which helps digest meat, as an after meal dessert. Eat meat along with vegetables that help digestion such as fingerroot, lemongrass, basil, and pepper.

Common cold. Eat food containing garlic, chilies, and sweet basil. Such dishes are *pad gaprao, tom jiw* (beef spicy soup), shrimp salad, and *gaeng pa*. Hot food helps stimulate a runny nose.

RECIPES

DIPS

Nam Prik Long Ruea (Hot Shrimp Paste Dip
with Crispy Fried Fish and Caramelized Pork)
Nam Prik Gapi (Spicy Dried Shrimp Dip)
Nam Prik Ong (Northern Thai Pork and Tomato Dip)
Lon Goong (Coconut Milk and Shrimp Dip)

Nam Prik Long Ruea

Hot Shrimp Paste Dip with Crispy Fried Fish and Caramelized Pork

A good nam prik long ruea should have pleasant fragrance. The flavour should not be spicy nor sweet. The texture should not be dry nor soggy. The colour should be brownish. The tip is to fry the ingredients well until fragrant. The paste can be stored in room temperature up to 3 days.

Nam prik
20g bird's eye chilies (25 chillies)
50g garlic
45g roasted shrimp paste in banana
  leaves
40g thinly sliced guttuferae
30g thinly sliced salacca palm
40g chopped bolo maka (hair removed)
30g lime juice
25g ground dried shrimps
100g palm sugar
30g vegetable oil

Finely chop 10g of garlic then set aside. Pound the rest of the 40g garlic with shrimp paste until they are finely mixed then add the chilies, guttuferae, salacca palm and bola maka, then continue pounding until all ingredients are well mixed together. Add palm sugar and lime juice and toss the mixture • Heat vegetable oil in the pan then add garlic and fry until fragrant. Add the paste mixture then reduce to low heat and continue to fry until fragrant. Add dried shrimps and stir well. Set aside the mixture into 60g portions then place in refrigerator.

Caramelized pork
200g boiled and diced (skinned)
  pork belly (½cm)
30g vegetable oil
70g palm sugar
30g fish sauce
30g sliced shallots

Heat vegetable oil over medium heat then add the shallots to fry. Add sugar and fish sauce, mix well then add diced pork belly. Reduce to low heat to caramelize the pork. Place the pork into a dish.

Crispy catfish
1 catfish, approximate weight of 300g
  (deboned steamed or grilled catfish)
2 cups of vegetable oil for deep-frying

Grate catfish into flakes and leave to air-dry. Heat vegetable oil over medium heat and gently sprinkle catfish flakes into the pan. Fry until golden then scoop out to drip excess oil and leave to cool. Place into a container and close the lid.

For 1 serving of nam prik long ruea
60g nam prik
25g caramelized pork
15g crispy catfish
⅓ salted egg yolk moulded into small balls
½ tsp thinly sliced pickled garlic
2 cucumbers, thickly sliced (1 cm)
2 cockroach berries, quartered
1 string bean, chopped (2 in.)
2 winged beans, diagonally chopped (2 in.)

Put 30g of water in the pan, add chili paste mixture, caramelized pork and stir well. Heat the pan over medium heat then add crispy catfish and stir well. Place the finished chili paste into a bowl, garnish with pickled garlic and salted egg yolk on top. Serve with fresh vegetables, cucumbers, cockroach berries, string bean and winged beans.

Tips

When pounding garlic and shrimp paste together, oil within the garlic will tone down the pungent smell of the shrimp paste and the garlic. Moreover, the chillies should be pounded coarsely. All ingredients should be stir-fried over low heat and caramelized pork and dried shrimp should be added during the stir-frying. Crispy catfish should be added last so the mixture does not dry up.

Nam prik long ruea can be stir-fried with rice and served with crispy catfish and fresh vegetables such as cucumbers, string beans and cockroach berries.

Nam Prik Gapi

Spicy Dried Shrimp Dip

A good nam prik gapi should be aromatic without pungent smell of shrimp paste. The texture should not be too thick but not runny, ready for dipping. The flavours should not be too sweet, not too salty and sour. And most important, nam prik gapi should not be too spicy.

Nam prik

25 bird's eye chilies
40g Thai garlic
60g roasted shrimp paste in banana
leaves
10g ground dried shrimp
30g chopped bolo maka, hair removed
80g palm sugar
80g lime juice

Pound garlic and shrimp paste until the garlic is all mashed • Add dried shrimps and bolo maka and continue pounding. Add crushed hot chilies and palm sugar, stir then add lime juice and blend well. All the flavours must come together, not too spicy or too sweet. This is to be served with fried mackerel, deep fried vegetables, boiled vegetables or fresh vegetables.
Deep fried vegetables Egg battered climbing wattles or eggplants
Boiled vegetables bamboo shoots, agasta flowers, cowslip creeper flowers, string beans

Egg battered climbing wattles and eggplants

300g shredded climbing wattles
1 eggplant
2 eggs
1 tbsp rice flour
2 cups vegetable oil for deep frying

Whisk eggs and rice flour together to make the batter mixture • Thinly slice the eggplants diagonally (approximately ¼ in.) • Heat vegetable oil over medium heat in a pan. As the oil is hot, dip the eggplants in the batter before placing in the pan. Deep-fry until golden on both sides then remove the vegetables and let them drain on greaseproof paper • Dip the climbing wattle in the batter mixture, separate into 2 portions and deep-fry both sides until golden. Remove the vegetables and let excess oil drip off. Cut the vegetables into bite size, approximately 5g.

Boiled vegetables

5 string beans
200g cowslip creeper flowers
10 winged beans
5 culms of farmed bamboo shoots
200g agasta flowers, pollens removed
½ cup thick coconut milk
1 tsp rice flour

Boil 2 cups of water and 2 tbsp of palm sugar in a pot. Add bamboo shoots then boil for 15-20 min. to remove the bitter taste. Remove the bamboo shoots and set aside • Boil 2 cups of water and 1 tsp of vegetable oil. Add agasta flowers in the boiling water, remove immediately when cooked and place in cold water. Boil the cowslip creeper flowers in the same manner. Boil the string beans and winged beans for 3 min. and remove immediately to place in cold water • Mix thick coconut milk and rice flour in the pot and warm over medium heat. As the mixture thickens remove from the stove. Use the coconut sauce to garnish over the boiled vegetables.

For **1** serving of nam prik gapi

80g nam prik gapi

1 fried mackerel, deboned

4 pieces of deep-fried eggplants

3 pieces of egg battered climbing wattles

6 boiled agasta flowers

20g boiled cowslip creeper flowers

4 winged beans, cut in 1½-in./piece

1 string bean, boiled and knotted

4 pieces of boiled and cut bamboo
   shoots (1½ in.)

3 tbsp thick coconut milk

Around a bowl of nam prik gapi, arrange all the boiled vegetables beautifully on the plate with coconut milk on top and
arrange deep-fried eggplants and climbing wattles on the
side. Serve with fried mackerel.

Tips

Preparation tips for nam prik gapi begin with the process of pounding garlic and shrimp paste in a well-blended manner to reduce the pungent smell of the two ingredients. Bird's eye chilies should be moderately crushed in order to maintain a balanced spicy flavor of the dish. Chilies can be added later to suit various preferences.

Sour mangoes can be used as a substitute for lime. Palm sugar is vital to this dish due to its mellow sweetness. The charisma of this dish lies at the varieties of vegetables which complement the flavour of nam prik gapi.

Thick coconut milk is used to minimize the bitterness of the vegetables and add more flavours. Nam prik gapi can also be eaten with fresh vegetables such as climbing wattles and cucumber.

Mackerel should be fried in hot oil until golden on both sides. The mackerel should be turned when it's fully cooked or its skin will peel off. Recommended oil to fry mackerel is palm oil due to its high boiling temperature in order to avoid burning.

Nam Prik Ong

Northern Thai Pork and Tomato Dip

Originally, this dish would use small tomatoes from northern part of Thailand which gives sour taste. If cooked with cherry tomatoes, tamarind juice should be added to bring out the natural tangy flavour. Nam prik ong can be used to cook other dishes such as kanom jeen nam ngeaw or fried rice. It is often served as a dip with pork cracking, fresh vegetables, cucumber or cabbage. It can also be served as spaghetti sauce or used as sandwich spread.

Nam prik ong

5 large dried chilies (25g)
15g thinly sliced lemongrass
30g thinly sliced shallots
10g chopped garlic
50g finely chopped pork
10g sea salt
30g fire grilled and pounded fermented
    beans (or substitute with 30g strained
    fermented soybeans)
200g diced cherry tomatoes
30g vegetable oil
15g finely chopped garlic

Remove all the seeds of the dried chillies and soak in water until tender. Then chop the chilies finely and pound with salt. Add lemongrass and pound well together. Add shallots and garlic and pound until the mixture is well blended together • Add fermented beans (or fermented soybeans) and pork, pound the ingredients together • Add tomatoes and stir well • Heat the vegetable oil over medium heat. As the oil is hot, add the garlic and fry until fragrant. Then add the pounded mixture and fry over low heat. Add 150g water and continue to stir until the mixture thickens. Taste and season as preferred. Add tamarind juice for more sour taste. Natural sour flavour can be derived from tomatoes. Place the cooked nam prik ong in a bowl.

For 1 serving of nam prik ong

80g nam prik ong
1 tbsp chopped spring onions
1 tbsp chopped coriander

Heat 30g water over low heat in a pan then add nam prik ong and stir well. As the mixture heats up, add chopped spring onions and coriander (set aside a small portion for garnish). Stir well • Place nam prik ong in a bowl and garnish with coriander. Serve with steamed pumpkin, boiled agasta flowers, boiled winged beans, and cucumber with pork crackling as a side dish.

Vegetables

3 pieces of steamed pumpkin (10g/piece)
40g boiled agasta flowers
2 diagonally cut boiled winged beans
    (1½ in./piece)
1 diagonally sliced fresh cucumber
    (1-cm thick)
Side dish: pork cracklings

Tips

Nam prik ong should be cooked until glossy but without excess oil on top. Tomatoes should blend well with consistent thickness and aromatic smell. The flavour should not be too spicy with sweetness from tomatoes. The colour of this dish should be tomato red.
Fermented beans are made from boiled and mashed soybeans, which goes to fermentation process and sun dried in circular sheets. It can be used as a substitute for shrimp paste. Fermented black soybeans has better fragrance than fermented white soybeans.

Lon Goong

Coconut Milk and Shrimp Dip

A good lon goong makes a great dip with strong prawn aroma and sweetness from coconut milk and shallots.

Lon goong
5 river prawns, 120g each
350g coconut milk
60g sliced shallots
30g concentrated tamarind juice
½ tsp fine sea salt
25g palm sugar

Peel and devein the river prawns, then remove heads and tails. Cut the prawns into small pieces then finely chop 150g of prawn meat. Remove dark sack in the prawn heads and excrete all the fat from the heads into a small bowl • Stir-fry the prawn fat with 1 tbsp of vegetable oil over low heat and set aside in a bowl • Heat mixture of coconut milk and chopped prawn meat over medium heat and bring to a boil then add shallots, palm sugar, tamarind juice and salt. Stir the mixture well, then add the stir-fried prawn fat. Taste and season.
Fresh vegetables cucumber, winged beans, cockroach berries, white turmeric, banana flowers
Side dish deep-fried battered shrimps

Deep-fried battered shrimps
200g small shrimps, antennas and
   rostrum removed
50g rice flour
10g all-purpose wheat flour
¼ tsp ground sea salt
250g palm oil for deep-frying

Mix rice flour, wheat flour and salt together then add 120g of cold water and stir until the batter reach the right consistency • Heat the oil over medium heat. When the oil is hot, dip the shrimps into the batter then gently fry the shrimps until golden. Scoop out and drain excess oil.

For 1 serving of lon goong
80g lon goong
10g thinly sliced shallots
2-3 green and red spur chilies, cut into
   1¼ cm
2 winged beans, cut into 1½ in. lenghts
2 cockroach berries, quartered
2 cucumbers, quartered, cut vertically
   into 1½ in. lenghts
20g thinly sliced banana flowers
3 pieces of thinly sliced green mango
5-6 pieces of thinly sliced white turmeric
   (¼ cm-thick)
4 deep-fried shrimps

Heat 30g water in a pot over medium heat, then add lon goong, shallots, chilies and stir well until the chilies are cooked • Place the mixture into a small bowl and garnish with coriander. Arrange all fresh vegetables and deep-fried shrimps around the plate to serve.

Tips
In the preparation, coconut milk and prawns should be mixed and stirred together before heating in order to avoid clumping.
Lon goong paste has smooth consistency with prawn texture and creaminess of shrimp fat.
Soak sliced banana flowers in lemon water to avoid darkening.

THAI SALADS

Yum Woon Sen (Vermicelli Spicy Salad)
Yum Nuea Yang (Grilled Beef Spicy Salad)
Yum Ka-Moay (Chicken Vegetables Salad)
Yum Som-O (Pomelo Salad)
Yum Tua-Pu (Winged Bean Salad)
Som Tum Goong Sod (Papaya Salad with Prawns)
Saeng-Wa Goong Pla Dook Foo (Grilled Prawn
   Salad with Fried Shredded Catfish)

Yum Woon Sen

Vermicelli Spicy Salad

Vermicelli in this dish should be chewy and not over-cooked. The salad must not be soggy, too sweet or too spicy. This dish should have well-balanced taste with no smell of vinegar. Salad dressing should be well blended or well pounded and sautéed over low heat to reduce the acidic smell of vinegar.

Salad dressing
50g red spur chilies, deseeded and finely chopped
20g coriander roots, finely chopped
30g garlic, finely chopped
50g sugar
10g ground sea salt
150g vinegar
25g lime juice

Pound the chilies, garlic, coriander roots and salt together • Place the mixture into a pot, add vinegar, sugar, 60g water and lime juice. Stir until the sugar dissolves • Heat the mixture over medium heat, stir until the sauce thickens. Taste and season. Set the dressing aside to cool and put in a container.

Other ingredients
80g vermicelli
100g white prawns (size 51/60)
100g pork loin
1 onion, 100g
2 tomatoes, 50g each
2 Chinese celery stalks, 50g each

Wash and devein the white prawns. Heat 1 cup of water in a pot and bring to a boil. Place the prawns (with shells) in the boiling water and when cooked, scoop out and place in cold water • Drain excess water then remove the shells and tails and cut the prawns in half lengthways • Boil 2 cups of water and add a pinch of salt. Place the pork loin in the boiling water and scoop out to drain excess water when cooked. Cut the pork loin into pieces of 5g • Deseed the tomatoes and cut into pieces of 5g. Deskin the onion and slice into 5g wedges • Boil one cup of water. Wash the vermicelli with clean water then place the vermicelli in boiling water, submerge for 3-4 min. Scoop out and place in cold water then drain excess water with a strainer. Wrap the vermicelli in muslin cloth to absorb all excess water. Use kitchen shears to cut the vermicelli into short strands.

For 1 serving of yum woon sen
60g cooked vermicelli
6 pieces of boiled pork loin, 30g
6 pieces of halved prawns
6 pieces of wedged onions
10g Chinese celery stalks, both stems and leaves, cut into short strands
5 pieces of wedged tomatoes
4 tbsp salad dressing, 60g

Stir and toss the pork, prawns and onions with 1 tbsp of the salad dressing in a mixing bowl • Add the vermicelli and the rest of the dressing, toss lightly. Then add the celery and tomatoes and toss again • Plate the vermicelli salad and serve.

Tips

To avoid over cooking, boil the vermicelli no more than 3-4 min. and immediately place in cold water after cooking. Use the strainer to drain excess water and wrap the vermicelli in muslin cloth to absorb the water. Tossing the pork, prawns and onions together can reduce the pungent smell of onions and increase good aroma to the meat.

Devein the prawns by using a toothpick to poke into the second abdominal segment of the shell and gently pick out the dark vein underneath the shell.

Yum Nuea Yang

Grilled Beef Spicy Salad

A good yum nuea yang dish should consist of tender beef without foul smell. Flavor varieties include spicy, sour, salty but not sweet. The dressing should absorb well into the meat so it is well moistened. The dish should have well-balanced flavors with crisp cucumbers.

Dressing

25g bird's eye chilies
30g finely chopped garlic
10g finely chopped coriander roots
70g fish sauce
80g lime juice
60g sugar

Pound bird's eye chilies, garlic and coriander roots together into a fine mixture • Add fish sauce and sugar, then heat the mixture over low heat. Stir until sugar dissolves. Remove from the stove • Add lime juice and stir well. Taste and season. The flavor should be well balanced between spicy, sour and salty with a tinge of sweetness. Set the dressing aside.

Other ingredients

300g rump beef steak
50g onion
1 lettuce
3 short cucumbers or 1 long cucumber
1 stalk coriander leaves
1 red spur chili

Pat the steak dry and place the steak on the grill with high heat to dry off the outer part, then reduce to medium heat and cook to preferred steak doneness: rare, medium or well done. Slice the steak against the grain into about 8g per piece • Peel an onion and cut in half. Slice into ½ cm thick wedges • Roughly tear the lettuce. Cut the short cucumbers in half and remove the seeds, then cut into ¼ cm-thick pieces. Or for long cucumbers, peel off the skin, remove the seeds and cut into the same size as the short cucumber.

For 1 serving of yum nuea yang

80g grilled beef
25g cucumber
15g onion
7-8 coriander leaves
2 lettuce leaves
Thinly sliced red spur chili
4 tbsp dressing (50-60g)

Toss grilled beef, onion and dressing in a mixing bowl • Add cucumber and top with coriander leaves and toss gently • Arrange the lettuce on the plate before plating the tossed grilled beef and garnish with red spur chili.

Tips

Rump steak should be stored in a refrigerator for 1 day before grilling to improve tenderness.
The beef should be grilled whole by using high heat to ensure that outer part of the steak is dry, then continue to grill with low heat (grilling with low heat from the beginning can cause moisture to drain from the meat which can reduce tenderness). Grilled beef should be left to cool before slicing to retain moisture and tenderness inside the steak. Degree of doneness suitable for grilled beef salad is medium to medium rare because the beef will continue to cook once it is tossed with the dressing (from lime juice). Overcooked beef does not absorb the dressing well.
Dressing should be simmered over low heat to achieve desirable taste and right consistency.

Yum Ka-Moay

Chicken Vegetables Salad

The dressing for this salad should be well balanced, not spicy or too sweet. It should have pleasant aroma with thick consistency, which should attach well with other ingredients.

Dressing
50g red spur chilies, deseeded, finely chopped
30g peeled garlic, finely chopped
15g coriander roots, finely chopped
10 peppercorns
50g sugar
60g fish sauce
60g lime juice
60g vinegar

Pound red chilies, garlic, coriander roots and peppercorns together. Add sugar, fish sauce and vinegar and stir well • Simmer the mixture in a pot over low heat for 10 min. Add lime juice and taste then continue to simmer for 2 min. and remove from the heat. Set the dressing aside.

Other ingredients
100g chicken breast
10 white prawns (size 51/60)
1 duck egg
1 lettuce
3 cucumbers, quartered, deseeded and thinly sliced into 5g/piece
1 onion (100g), sliced into ½ cm thick wedges
1 stalk of coriander, for coriander leaves
1 stalk of lemongrass, crushed
80g mint leaves
1 red spur chili, thinly sliced

Heat 2 cups of water in a pot and bring to a boil. Pound a stalk of lemongrass and add to the boiling water. Add chicken breast and cooked until done. Leave the chicken breast to cool before cutting into 5 grams/piece • Wash and devein the prawns. Add the prawns (shells intact) to boiling water, when cooked, scoop out and immediately place in cold water. Once the prawns are cooled, remove the shells, heads and tails and cut in half across the back • Boil 1 cup of water and add a pinch of salt. Boil the egg for 15 min. and keep stirring until the egg is cooked to keep the yolk in the center. Once cooked, immediately place in cold water.

For 1 serving of yum ka-moay
40g boiled chicken, 8 pieces
4 pieces of halved prawns
1 vertically sliced boiled egg (4-5 pieces)
2 roughly torn lettuce leaves
45g cucumbers
5-6 mint leaves
25g onion
Thinly slice red spur chili
5-6 coriander leaves
60g dressing (4-5 tbsp)

Toss the onion, chicken and prawns together in a mixing bowl • Add 2 tbsp of the dressing, toss well then add cucumber. Add 1 tbsp of dressing and toss well • Add lettuce and mint leaves, toss and plate the mixture. Arrange boiled egg on the side and garnish with coriander leaves and red spur chili.

Tips

Onion should be tossed with chicken and prawns to reduce the onion, pungent smell and increase the pleasant smell of the meat of this dish.

Cucumbers should be deseeded to reduce the liquid in the salad, which may cause salad to become bland. If you are using long cucumber, it should be soaked in cold water to retain the crispness before peeling and deseeding.

The dressing should be gradually added for the flavors to spread evenly when tossed. If you are using seafood as your meat portion, add 5g of chopped bird's eye chilies, 5g of chopped garlic and 100g of salad dressing.

If you do not place the boiled egg in cold water immediately, it may cause darkening around the yolk and unpleasant smell.

Yum Som-O

Pomelo Salad

Good yum som-o dressing should have well balanced flavors, which is not too spicy, sweet or salty. The dressing should soak well on the pomelo flesh and well moisture with aromatic scent. The salad dressing should be simmered over low heat. Large dried chilies are ideal for this dish and avoid using fresh spur chilies.

Dressing

3 large dried chillies (15g) deseeded, pan roasted, finely crushed
50g grilled crispy fish, pounded
80g pan roasted chopped shallots
30g pan roasted chopped garlic
220g palm sugar
200g fish sauce
200g boiled tamarind juice

Pound dried chilies, shallots and garlic together until the mixture is well blended. Add fish sauce, sugar and tamarind juice and stir until the sugar dissolves • Place the mixture in a pot and stir over low heat. Continue stirring then add crispy fish and simmer until the mixture thickens. Taste and season. Set the dressing aside in a bowl.

Other ingredients

300g pomelo flesh
10 white shrimps (size 51/60)
50g pan roasted grated coconut
50g coarsely pounded peanuts
100g chopped shallots
½ cup vegetable oil
1 red spur chili, thinly sliced
3-4 kaffir lime leaves, thinly sliced

Gently break the pomelo flesh into small segments • Wash and de-vein the shrimps. Place the whole shrimps into boiling water, scoop out and soak in cold water when cooked. Remove the shells, heads and tails. Thinly slice the shrimps diagonally • Heat vegetable oil over low heat. When the oil is warm, add chopped shallots and stir at all times. As the shallots begin to turn golden, remove from the pan and leave the shallots to drain off excess oil.

For 1 serving of yum som-o

120g pomelo
30g boiled shrimps
3-4 tbsp dressing
1 tbsp roasted peanuts
1 tbsp roasted coconut
1 tbsp fried shallots
1 tsp red spur chili
3 lettuce leaves (or 3 wildbetal leaves)
1 tsp kaffir lime leaves

Add pomelo and shrimps into the mixing bowl and toss lightly with dressing. Add roasted coconut, roasted peanuts and toss. Finally add ½ tbsp of fried shallots and toss • Arrange lettuce or wildbetal leaves on one side of the plate and then add the tossed pomelo salad in the middle. Garnish with fried shallots, thinly sliced chili and kaffir lime leaves on top.

Tips

Pomelo flesh should be firm, dry and has large pulps. Ideally, suitable pomelo varieties for this dish are Kao-yai, Kao-puang and Kao-sa-ad. Smaller pulps and segments are great for tossing with salad dressing. (The Thong-dee pomelo is not a suitable variety for this dish due to the juicy flesh which become soggy when tossed with dressing.) Pomelo flesh should be tossed with dressing before adding roasted coconut and peanuts. The roasted coconut and peanuts are added last because they will absorb all dressing, resulting to bland flavors.

Yum Tua-Pu

Winged Beans Salad

An ideal yum tua-pu dish is composed of green cooked winged beans, aromatic dressing, well moisture but not soggy texture with well-balanced flavors. This dish has stronger flavors than Pomelo Salad. Coconut milk should not be topped over the salad when plating this dish.

Dressing

4 large dried chilies, cut into small pieces, pan roasted (20g)
100g pan roasted chopped shallots
60g pan roasted chopped garlic
100g sugar
80g fish sauce
80g lime juice

Pound dried chillies, shallots and garlic together into a fine mixture. Add fish sauce and sugar and blend the mixture together • Place the mixture in a pot over low heat until the sugar dissolves. Add lime juice and stir. Taste and season for well-balanced flavors, not too overly salty and spicy. Set the dressing aside into a bowl.

Other ingredients

300g winged beans
100g pork rump steak
50g grated roasted coconut
100g of slice shallots
1 thinly sliced red spur chili
50g coarsely pounded peanuts
100g thick coconut milk (pre-heated)

Wash the winged beans. Heat 2 cups of water, add 1 tsp of vegetable oil and bring to a boil. Add the winged beans and make sure they are submerged under the water. Boil for 2 min. and immediately place in cold water. After the beans cool down, drain excess water then cut into ¼ cm pieces • Boil 2 cups of water and add a pinch of salt. Boil the pork until cooked, then remove from water. Cut the pork into 5g pieces • Heat ¼ cup of vegetable oil over low heat. As the oil heats up add chopped shallots and stir at all times. As the shallots begin to golden, remove from the pan and leave to drain excess oil.

For 1 serving of yum tua-pu

120g winged beans
10 pieces of cooked pork, 50g
3-4 tbsp dressing
1 tbsp fried shallots
1 tbsp roasted coconut
1 tbsp roasted peanuts
1 tbsp thick coconut milk
1 tsp thinly sliced red spur chili

Toss winged beans and pork with coconut milk in a mixing bowl • Gradually add dressing and toss the mixture together. Add roasted coconut, peanuts and fried shallots and toss. Plate the mixture and garnish with red spur chili.

Tips

Winged beans should be boiled in water over high heat and pressed to submerge all the beans. Boiling time should not exceed 3 min. to avoid the winged beans to darken. When the winged beans are cooked, they should be placed in cold water immediately to prevent the beans to continue cooking, which will cause the color to change. Boil the winged beans just before using them. It is not recommended to store the cut winged beans, ideally they should be kept as whole beans

Pre-heated coconut milk should be heating until fragrant. It is used to toss with winged beans and to tenderize the pork, as well as enhancing the flavors.

Som Tum Goong Sod

Papaya Salad with Prawns

A good som tum dish composes of crisp papaya, not soggy with well-balanced flavors. Tangy flavor from lime juice and bitterness from lime zest enhances the flavor of this dish. Add fresh bird's eye chilies on the side for more hotness. Chili powder is not recommended because it lacks fragrance and flavor.

Dressing

3 large dried chilies, deseeded, soaked
   in water, finely chopped (15g)
100g boiled thick tamarind juice
200g palm sugar
120g fish sauce
20 peppercorns
30g finely chopped garlic
80-100g lime juice

Other ingredients

300g green papaya, finely chopped into
   short strands
4 boiled prawns, shells, heads and tails
   removed, cut into small pieces (50g)
1 lime, cut into small pieces, with skin
   and flesh
100g dried shrimps, washed and dried,
   pounded into fluffy powdered texture
Lettuce and wildbetal leaves

Pound chilies, peppercorn and garlic together until the mixture is well blended • Transfer the mixture into a pot, add fish sauce, sugar and tamarind paste and stir. Simmer over low heat until the mixture thickens and remove from the stove. Add lime juice and stir. Taste and season for well-balanced flavors. Set the mixture aside in a bowl.

For 1 serving of som tum goong sod

150g chopped papaya
2 boiled prawns
10g chopped lime
1 tbsp powdered dried shrimps
3 red and green bird's eye chilies
3-4 tbsp som-tum dressing
1 lettuce leaf
2-3 wildbetal leaves

Pound chilies in the mortar then add green papaya and pound gently. As the papaya softens add som-tum dressing and toss the mixture together. Then add powdered dried shrimps, followed by chopped lime and toss. Finally, add boiled prawns and toss. Arrange wildbetal and lettuce leaves on the side of the plate, then add the salad to the plate.

Tips

Ideally, large and round papaya fruit is recommended over long papaya fruit because it has crispy flesh. Soak whole papaya in cold water to enhance the meat crispness. Peel the papaya and wash to remove fruit enzymes. Chop the papaya flesh into short and thin strands or use a shredder to shred the papaya into short strands not more than 1½ inch long. Wrap the papaya strands in thin white cloth.

Papaya should be gently pounded in the mortar, as is soften it can absorb the dressing well. If the papaya is tossed, it will be flavorless.

Dried shrimps should be washed and air dried before pounded into fluffy powdered texture. If the dried shrimp is placed in the grinder, it will become into dried powdered form.

Lime juice should be added gradually bit by bit. In some seasons, lime juice can be very sour. If the tamarind juice is too sweet, it can be seasoned with lime juice.

Saeng-Wa Goong Pla Dook Foo

Grilled Prawn Salad with Fried Crispy Catfish

This dish has its origin from fish kidney spicy salad. They have the same preparation and ingredients, as well as flavors which are salty, sour and a little sweet. Ginger gives a hot kick in this dish, while the lemongrass and shallots provide aromatic scent. Saeng-wa salad is moist from the dressing, while the fried catfish prevents the dish from being too soggy.

Saeng-wa dressing
120g fish sauce
80g sugar
100g boiled thick tamarind juice
80g lime juice

Mix all ingredients in a pot and simmer over low heat for approximately 15 min. Taste and season for well-balanced flavors between salty, sour and sweet. As the mixture thickens, remove from heat and set aside in a bowl.

Other Ingredients
4 river prawns, 125g each
30g thinly sliced shallots
1 finely sliced red spur chili
3 thinly sliced lemongrass
50g young ginger, peeled and finely
   shredded
5 kaffir lime leaves
1 steamed catfish, 500g
3 cups of palm oil for deep-frying

Grill and peel the prawns. Use a fork to shred the meat into puffy texture • Soak the sliced shallots, lemongrass and ginger in water mixed with lime juice to prevent discoloration and retain their vibrant color • Remove midrib and thinly slice the kaffir lime leaves • Remove the meat from the steamed catfish and set aside and leave to remove some moisture, then separate the fish into 2 portions for frying. Heat the oil over high heat in a wok. As the oil is hot, sprinkle catfish meat and fry until golden. Remove from the wok to drain excess oil. Set aside.

For 1 serving of saeng-wa kung
100g prawn meat
30g sliced lemongrass
30g sliced shallots
30g sliced ginger
1 tbsp sliced kaffir lime leaves
50g fried catfish
1 tbsp thinly sliced red spur chilies
3-4 tbsp saeng-wa dressing

Toss prawn meat, shallots, lemongrass and ginger together in a mixing bowl • Slowly add the dressing bit by bit and toss lightly. Sprinkle kaffir lime leaves and red spur chilies over and toss lightly (leave some for garnish). Finally, add the fried catfish and toss well • Plate the mixture and garnish with kaffir lime leaves and red chilies. Serve with cucumber, lettuce and string beans.

Tips
Shredded prawn meat can soak up the dressing better than sliced prawns. Catfish should be deep-fried in palm oil over high heat for golden fluffy texture. Steamed catfish is preferred over grilled one because grilled catfish can be too dry and will not fluff up when deep-fried.
Spicy salad is usually served with fresh vegetables such as cucumber, string beans or cockroach berries. They can also be served in crispy cups as snacks or served as a cocktail dish.

SOUPS

Tom Yum Goong (Clear Prawn Soup)
Tom Kha Gai (Chicken in Coconut Milk Soup)
Tom Som Pla Tu (Mackerel in Tamarind Soup)
Tom Jiw (Beef Spicy Soup)
Gaeng Liang Goong Sod (Thai Mixed Vegetable Soup with Prawns)
Gaeng Jued Sam Gasat (Chicken, Pork, Shrimp Soup)

Tom Yum Goong

Clear Prawn Soup

Tom yum goong should be served warm. Pleasant aroma of this dish is derived from the lemongrass, the kaffir lime leaves and prawns. The tom yum soup should be clear with orange shades from shrimp fats. The dominant flavor of this dish is sour, followed by the sweetness from the stock with a touch of salty flavor. The lemongrass should be cooked and the prawns should be tender.

Chicken stock
1½ kg whole chicken bone
30g coriander roots
70g shallots
1 stalk of lemongrass
2,500g water (10 cups)

Wash the whole chicken bone, remove all the fats and chop into big chunks. Put water into a pot and add the bones, leave to soak for 5 min • Heat the pot with the chicken bone over low heat then add crushed coriander roots, crushed shallots and crushed lemongrass stalk. Simmer for 30 min. (Add some shrimp shells if available) • Remove the chicken bones and strain the soup for chicken stock.

Tom yum stock
75-90g fish sauce
75-90g lime juice
1,500g chicken stock (6 cups)

Boil chicken stock in a pot then add fish sauce. Add lime juice and taste to season. Set the stock aside.

Other ingredients
6 giant freshwater prawns (150g each)
30g vegetable oil
4-5 kaffir lime leaves
2 stalks of thinly sliced lemongrass
15 bird's eye chilies, stems removed

Wash the prawns and remove the dark sac from head while preserving the shrimp fat in a small bowl. Remove the shells, heads and tails. Cut almost through the curved back portion of the prawns and remove the veins. Parboil the prawns in the stock until they are 70% cooked • Heat the oil over low heat, then add the prawns as the oil is hot. Stir-fry until fragrant then set aside the prawns in a bowl • Wash and thinly slice the lemongrass and leave to soak in clean water with lime juice.

For **1** serving of tom yum goong
2 parboiled prawns
250g tom yum stock
1 shredded kaffir lime leaf (4 pieces)
3 crushed bird's eye chilies
1 tbsp sliced lemongrass
2 tsp shrimp fats

Heat tom yum stock in a pot then add lemongrass as the stock is boiling • Add the prawns, kaffir lime leaf, shrimp fats. Turn off the heat then pour the soup into a bowl to serve.

Tips

Parboiling the prawns in the stock will enhance the aroma of the stock. Adding prawns' shells and heads can enhance the flavors of the stock to be fragrant, sweet and well-balanced.

Sliced lemongrass should be soaked in water with lime juice (1 cup of water for 2 tsp of lime juice) to prevent discoloration. Adding lemongrass and fish sauce while the stock is boiling helps bring out the pleasant fragrant of the lemongrass and can prevent fish sauce from smelling too fishy.

The ideal kaffir lime leaves should be moderately mature since leaves that are overly mature can give out stronger fragrance and can be too tough to eat, while younger leaves are not aromatic.

Galangal is not an ingredient for this dish because of its bitter taste, which may reduce the aroma of the prawns.

Chilies are added later in order to prevent over spicing the dish.

Tom Kha Gai

Chicken in Coconut Milk Soup

A good tom kha gai dish consists of tender chicken meat with pleasant aroma of galangal and lemongrass. The galangal should be cooked otherwise it will taste bitter. The soup should not be too thick and it should have a touch of sour flavor.

Tom kha soup

250g thick coconut milk
1,000g thin coconut milk (500g thick coconut milk and 500g water)
15g sugar
60-70g fish sauce
60-70g lime juice
50g mature galangal

Boil thin coconut milk in a pot, then add crushed galangal and continue to simmer over low heat for 10 min. Scoop out the galangal • Add sugar, fish sauce, lime juice and thick coconut milk. Taste and season for a touch of sour flavor. Remove from stove.

Other ingredients

300g chicken breast
100g young galangal
2 stalks of lemongrass
15 green and red bird's eye chilies, stems removed
4-5 kaffir lime leaves
250g diluted coconut milk (60g thick coconut milk and 190g water)

Wash and pat the chicken dry. Slice the chicken across the meat grain, 5g per piece. Heat the thin coconut milk in a pot, add the chicken and boil for 3 min. then remove the chicken meat • Thinly slice the lemongrass and soak in water and lime juice • Peel the galangal and cut into thin slices. If the galangal is mature, cut into slices then cut into long strips. Soak the galangal in water and lime juice.

For 1 serving of tom kha gai

250g tom kha soup
10 pieces chicken (50g)
3-4 crushed bird's eye chilies
1 kaffir lime leaf (torn into 4 pieces)
15g sliced galangal
1½ tsp sliced lemongrass

Heat the tom kha soup in a pot then add galangal and lemongrass • Add chicken meat, kaffir lime leaf, chilies and turn up the heat. Keep boiling for 15 seconds. Serve in a bowl.

Tips

Coconut milk must be stirred at all time over the stove, avoid using high heat to prevent clumping. Mature galangal is used in order to effectively diffuse its fragrance into the soup. It helps relieve abdominal distention and suitable for those avoiding fatty foods. Recommended storing instruction for tom kha soup is refrigeration over freezer. Boiling chicken meat in coconut milk makes the meat tender and fragrant.

Tom Som Pla-tu

Mackerel in Tamarind Soup

The soup should have pleasant aroma with thick consistency (but not creamy). The dominant flavor is sweet with the taste of ginger to balance the overall taste. Hotness of the ginger enhances flavor of the dish. This herb helps keep the fish meat intact and reduces fishy smell of the mackerel.

Tom som soup

1,250g water
15g finely sliced coriander roots
15 peppercorns
50g finely sliced shallots
20g concentrated tamarind juice
80g palm sugar
15g fish sauce
10g shrimp paste

Pound the coriander roots, peppercorns and shallots together until they are all well blended. Add the shrimp paste and pound the mixture together • Heat the water in a pot over medium heat and dissolve the paste mixture then bring to a boil. Remove from heat • Add fish sauce, tamarind juice and sugar. Taste and season for sweet then sour.

Other ingredients

3 large mackerels, approximately
  80-100g each
50 sliced young ginger, soaked in water
  mixed with lime juice
3 stalks of spring onion, chopped into
  1 in. pieces
2 red spur chilies, sliced diagonally
2 stalks of coriander, coarsely chopped

Wash and gut the mackerel, remove the heads and tails. Score the fish on both sides • Boil the water in a pot and parboil the mackerel to 70% then scoop out.

For 1 serving of tom som pla-tu

1 mackerel
250g tom som soup
15g sliced ginger
1 stalk of chopped spring onion
3 pieces of sliced red spur chili
1 tbsp coarsely chopped coriander

Heat the tom som soup over medium heat and bring to a boil. Add ginger and stir until fragrant. Add the mackerel and turn up the heat and bring to a boil again before removing from the heat • Add spring onion and red chili. Serve warm in a bowl and garnish with coriander.

Tips

Parboiling the mackerel to about 70% can help prevent fishy smell and keeps the fish meat intact. Young ginger is the recommended ingredient for this dish because of its mild taste. Tamarind juice and fish sauce should be added when the soup is boiling to enhance the aroma.

Tom Jiw

Beef Spicy Soup

Tom jiw soup is considered a dish for cold relief. It has strong aroma from kaffir lime leaves and sweet basil with sweetness from shallots. The soup should be clear with strong sour flavor. The sweet potatoes should not be over cooked and mushy. The beef should be cooked and tender.

Tom jiw stock
500g flank steak
6-7 cups of water
40g tamarind juice
30g lime juice
40g fish sauce

Heat the water in a pot and the whole flank steak, then lower the heat to simmer until the beef is cooked and tender. Remove the beef and strain 5 cups of stock • Heat the stock in a pot and bring to a boil. Add fish sauce, tamarind juice and lime juice. Taste and season for strong flavors of sour and salty.

Other ingredients
1 sweet potato (150g), boiled, peeled
  and cut into 1 in. cubes of 10g each
Beef, cut into 1 in. cubes of 15g each
100g sweet basil leaves
100g holy basil leaves
100g sliced shallots
15 bird's eye chilies, stems removed

For 1 serving of tom jiw
250g tom jiw stock
4 cubes of boiled beef
3 cubes of boiled sweet potato
10 sweet basil leaves
10 holy basil leaves
4 crushed bird's eye chilies
20g sliced shallots

Heat tom jiw stock over medium heat, then add the shallots to cook • Add sweet potatoes, beef and continue to heat the soup • Add sweet basil leaves, basil leaves and bird's eye chilies. Increase to high heat and continue to cook for 15 seconds. Serve in a bowl.

Tips
The beef should be cooked and simmer whole for tenderness and full flavor. Cooking the beef that has been cut into small pieces will cause them to shrink and become chewy. A fresh piece of steak should be washed clean and refrigerated overnight before cooking. The enzyme in the beef will help tenderize the meat.

Gaeng Liang Goong Sod

Thai Mixed Vegetable Soup with Prawns

Gaeng liang soup has a slightly thick consistency because of prawn meat. The soup is fragrant with vegetables that are not overcooked with a bit of spicy flavor from peppercorns. The flavor is not overly spicy and does not smell of shrimp paste.

Gaeng liang stock

1,250g water
15g fish sauce
40g sliced shallots
17 peppercorns
15g shrimp paste
50g boiled prawn meat

Pound peppercorns and shallots together into fine mixture. Add shrimp paste and pound until the mixture is well blended. Add prawn meat, pound moderately • Heat water in a pot then add the pounded mixture and adjust to medium heat. Add fish sauce and taste to season for well-balanced flavors.

Other ingredients

20 white prawns (size 50/60)
100g angled gourd, peeled and cut into
   10g pieces
100g corn seeds
100g ivy gourd leaves (edible leaves only)
100g hoary basil leaves

Peel the prawn shells, remove the heads, tails and dark veins across the backs. Parboil the prawns in boiling water until they are cooked to about 70%.

For 1 serving of gaeng liang goong sod

1 cup of gaeng liang stock
3 parboiled prawns
5 pieces of cut angled gourd (50g)
2 tbsp corn seeds (30g)
¼ cup ivy gourd leaves (30g)
9-10 hoary basil leaves

Boil the stock in a pot then add angled gourds • Add corn seeds and stir. Add ivy gourd leaves and hoary basil leaves then adjust to high heat. Add the prawns and stir. Pour the soup in a bowl, ready to be served.

Tips

Vegetables used in this dish should be those with cold characteristics such as angled gourd (also known as angled luffa, Chinese okra, and ringed gourd), ivy gourd or bottle gourd. This is to balance out the hotness from the peppercorns.
Avoid using dried shrimps due to their pungent scent.
Hoary basil leaves enhances the smell and flavor, while peppercorns gives out the ideal level of hotness of this soup dish.
Bird's eye chilies or other types of chilies are not used as ingredients for this dish due to their strong hot flavors.

Gaeng Jued Sam Gasat

Chicken, Pork, Shrimp Soup

The soup should be clear with pleasant aroma and sweet flavor from the carrots. Bundled pork, chicken and prawns should be a bite size. Chinese white radish and carrot are perfectly cooked.

Soup stock
1,250g chicken stock
30g fish sauce
10g finely chopped garlic
10g finely chopped coriander roots
5 peppercorns

Pound coriander roots, peppercorns and garlic together into a fine mixture • Boil chicken stock in a pot then add the mixture and stir well. Add fish sauce then taste to season.

Other ingredients
100g pork loin
20 white prawns (size 70/80)
100g chicken breast
1 salted pickled turnip head, sliced into thin 6 in. long strings
5 stalks of spring onion
1 carrot, boiled unpeeled
1 Chinese white radish, boiled unpeeled

Cut the pork and chicken into pieces of 2½ inches (3g each). Peel the prawn shells, remove the heads, tails and dark veins across the backs • Tie the pork, chicken and prawns tightly together with the turnip strings. Parboil the meat in boiling water for 1 min. • Peel the carrot. Carve the radish into sections • Cut the carrot and radish into pieces of ½ cm thick then cut in halves. Boil the vegetables in the stock and scoop to set aside in a bowl. Cut the spring onions into 1-inch-long pieces.

For 1 serving of gaeng jued sam gasat
1½ cup of soup stock
4 bundles of pork, chicken and prawn meat
4 pieces of Chinese white radish
3 pieces of carrot
1 stalk of spring onion

Boil the stock in a pot, add the radish and carrots then reduce to low heat for 1 min. Add the bundled meat • Adjust to high heat then add spring onion and stir. Remove from the heat and pour into a bowl, serve warm.

Tips
Boiling the carrots and fresh white radish in the stock will enhance the natural sweet flavor to the soup. Salted pickled turnip makes the soup tastier, however the turnip should be washed with clean water before cooking.

CURRIES

Gaeng Pet Ped Yang (Roasted Duck Red Curry)
Gaeng Keaw Wan Gai (Chicken Green Curry)
Gaeng Kua Supparod (Shrimp Curry with Pineapple)
Choo Chee Pla (Curry-Fried Fish)
Panang Gai (Chicken Panang Curry)
Gaeng Massaman Gai (Chicken Massaman Curry)
Gaeng Pet Gai (Chicken Red Curry)
Gaeng Garee Gai (Chicken Yellow Curry)
Gaeng Nuea Prik Kee Noo (Beef Spicy Green Curry)
Hor Mok Pla Chon (Steamed Fish with Curry Paste in Banana Leaf Cups)

Gaeng Pet Ped Yang

Roasted Duck Red Curry

The curry should have thick consistency and pleasant fragrance with a bit of oil. The flavors are well balanced and not too spicy. The pineapples and the pea eggplants are cooked without darkened skin. The cherry tomatoes are cooked but not mushy.

Roasted duck red curry base

100g roasted duck red curry paste
  (see page 153)
250g thick coconut milk
875g diluted coconut milk (440g thick
  coconut milk mixed with 435g water)
25g fish sauce
5g ground sea salt
10g sugar
30g vegetable oil
250g pineapple juice (no added sugar)

Heat the vegetable oil in a pan over medium heat. As the oil is hot, add the curry paste and stir-fry until fragrant. Gradually add thick coconut milk and keep stirring. Add fish sauce, sugar and salt then continue to stir. Transfer the mixture in a pot • Continue to heat the mixture in a pot, gradually add the thin coconut milk then add the pineapple juice. Bring to a boil for 1 min. and remove from the heat.

Other ingredients

400g roasted duck meat
250g diluted coconut milk (60g thick
  coconut milk mixed with 190g water)
200g pineapple meat (cut into 10g
  pieces)
100g pea eggplants (stems removed)
100g Thai Sida tomatoes
4-5 kaffir lime leaves
100g sweet basil leaves

Cut the roasted duck into 8-gram pieces. Heat the thin coconut milk in a pot then boil the roasted duck for 5 min. Scoop out the duck and set aside • Boil 2 cups of water in a pot, add 1 tsp of vinegar and 1 tsp of vegetable oil. Boil the pea eggplants for 3 min. and scoop out to soak in cold water immediately. As the eggplants cool, scoop out and drain excess water • Halve the tomatoes horizontally.

For 1 serving of gaeng pet ped yang

190g roasted duck red curry base
10 pieces of roasted duck
5 pieces of pineapple
8 pea eggplants
7 sweet basil leaves
4 halved Sida tomatoes
1 shredded kaffir lime leaf (4 pieces)

Heat the curry base in a pot, add the pineapple when the curry is warm then continue to heat for 30 seconds • Add the roasted duck and bring to a boil. Add the pea eggplants, kaffir lime leaves, tomatoes and sweet basil leaves and stir well. Remove from the heat and serve in a bowl.

Tips

Ideal pineapple for this dish should have bright green skin with a tinge of sour flavor. Canned pineapple juice should not have added sugar. Pineapple juice it can help balance out the flavor of the soup.
Duck meat should be moist with the curry soup when bitten.
Cutting the tomatoes horizontally helps retain their texture when cooked.

Gaeng Keaw Wan Gai

Chicken Green Curry

The curry should have slightly think consistency with coconut milk well blended in the curry and not floating on the surface. The color of this curry dish should be green with aromatic fragrant from spices. The chicken meat is tender, while the eggplants are cooked but their skin not darkened. The overall taste is well-balanced, not too sweet or too hot.

Green curry base

100g green curry paste (see page 152)
30g vegetable oil
45g fish sauce
25g palm sugar
250g thick coconut milk
875g thin coconut milk (440g thick coconut milk mixed with 435g water)

Heat the oil in a pan over medium heat. Add the green curry paste as the oil is hot and stir-fry for 2 min. Gradually add all the coconut cream and continue stirring until the fat appears (do not stir-fry until the oil disintegrates) • Transfer the mixture into a pot then add the fish sauce. Divide the thick coconut milk into 3 portions and gradually add all portions one by one. Add sugar and taste to season. Adjust to high heat for 1 min. then remove from the heat.

Other ingredients

500g chicken breast
250g thin coconut milk (60g thick coconut milk mixed with 190g water)
5 kaffir lime leaves
100g pea eggplants, stems removed
50g sweet basil leaves
1 red spur chili, sliced diagonally

Wash and pat the chicken dry then slice the chicken across the grain into 5-gram pieces. Heat the thin coconut milk in a pot over medium heat, as the coconut milk is hot, boil the chicken meat for 3 min. Scoop out the meat and set aside in a bowl • Boil 2 cups of water with 1 tsp of vegetable oil and 1 tsp of vinegar over high heat. Place the pea eggplants in the boiling water and keep the eggplants submerged for 3-4 min. Scoop out and soak in cold water immediately. As the eggplants cool down, drain excess water.

For 1 serving of gaeng keaw wan gai

190g green curry base
15 pieces of chicken meat
10 pea eggplants
1 shredded kaffir lime leaf (4 pieces)
7-8 sweet basil leaves
2 pieces sliced red spur chili

Heat green curry base and chicken meat in a pot over medium heat and bring to a boil. Add kaffir lime leaf, sweet basil leaves, pea eggplants, and red chili. Adjust to high heat and cook for another 2 seconds. Serve in a bowl.

Tips

If the curry paste does not have nice green color, crush some chili leaves or coriander leaves, then squeeze their juice. Strain the green juice and add it to the curry paste while stir-frying with coconut milk in order to enhance the green color.

To improve the fragrance of ready-made curry paste, add a mixture of pounded coriander roots, garlic and cumin.

Refrain from burning the mixture while roasting since it can darken the color of the curry. Stir-frying the curry paste with oil will enhance the fragrance and will help pre-cook the mixture (uncooked mixture can have bitter taste).

Adding thick coconut milk while cooking must be done gradually bit by bit. Pouring the coconut milk all at once can cause it to curdle and rise to the surface.

Green curry base should be stored in a container and refrigerated. The curry should be at room temperature before used for cooking because cold green curry base will cause the coconut cream to curdle and float to the surface.

The chicken meat should be pre-cooked or pre-boiled in thin coconut milk in order to prevent thinning of the soup consistency. The chicken meat should be tender without foul smell. Adding some vinegar in the water for boiling the pea eggplants can help retain the fresh color and keep the flesh intact.

Gaeng Kua Supparod

Shrimp Curry with Pineapple

The curry should have red orange color without any curdles floating on the surface. It is neither too sweet nor too hot but has aromatic smell of the pineapple. The curry soup consistency is slightly thick.

Chili curry base

100g chili curry paste (see page 154)
250g thick coconut milk
1,000g thin coconut milk (500g thick coconut milk mixed with 500g water)
40g boiled tamarind juice
30g palm sugar
50g fish sauce
40g vegetable oil

Heat the vegetable oil in a pan over medium heat, add the curry paste to stir-fry until fragrant. Gradually add the thick coconut milk bit by bit and keep stirring • Add the fish sauce and palm sugar then gradually pour in all the diluted coconut milk bit by bit. Add the tamarind juice, reduce the heat and continue to simmer for 2 min. Taste and season for well-balanced flavors. Remove from heat and place the curry base in a bowl.

Other ingredients

1 pineapple (green skin, about 1 kg)
4-5 kaffir lime leaves
500g white prawns (size 50/60)
250g thin coconut milk (60g thick coconut milk mixed with 190g water)

Wash the pineapple and slice off the skin. Cut into 1-inch thick chunks and remove the cores. Cut the pineapple in halves and then into small long wedges • Peel off the prawn shells, remove the heads, tails, cut along the outer edge of the prawns' backs and remove the veins. • Boil the thin coconut milk in a pot. Parboil the prawns in the boiling coconut milk to about 70% then immediately scoop out.

For 1 serving of gaeng kua supparod

200g chili curry base
1 shredded kaffir lime leaf (4 pieces)
3 cooked prawns
80g pineapple

Heat the curry base in a pot and as the curry heats up add the pineapple then adjust to medium heat for 30 seconds and add the prawns. Adjust to high heat and add kaffir lime leaf and continue to boil for 10 seconds. Remove from heat and serve in a bowl.

Tips

Shrimp curry with pineapple dish uses slightly sour pineapple meat, which are cut into small, long wedges, rather than in cubes. The pineapple should be cooked first before adding the prawns.
Parboiling the prawns in the coconut milk makes the prawn tender.
Alternatively, you can also use very ripe wax gourd as an ingredient by cutting the gourd into 10g pieces. Pre-boil the gourds in the coconut milk for tenderness. Added raw in the curry, the gourds will not become tender and do not absorb the sauce well. Adding small amount of tamarind juice can enhance the flavor of this curry dish.

Choo Chee Pla

Curry-Fried Fish

The curry base of this dish has orange red color because it does not consist of coriander seeds and cumin. The curry is fragrant from kaffir lime zest with slightly thick consistency. Dominant flavor of this dish is sweetness from coconut milk. The curry sauce should have fat moderately blended in without any presence of curdles on the surface. Another name for curry-fried dish is sweet curry due to the sweet flavor from coconut milk.

Choo chee curry base
100g choo chee curry paste (see page 152)
750g thin coconut milk (250g thick coconut milk diluted with 500g water)
125g thick coconut milk
45g fish sauce
50g palm sugar
30g vegetable oil

Heat the oil in a pan over medium heat and as the oil is hot add the curry paste and stir-fry until fragrant then add the fish sauce and stir well • Gradually add all the thick coconut milk bit by bit and stir-fry until oil begins to separate. Transfer the mixture into a pot and put over medium heat. Slowly add all the diluted coconut milk bit by bit. Add the sugar and stir well then taste to season. Remove from heat and set aside in a bowl.

Other ingredients
500g sea bass fillet
10g finely sliced kaffir lime leaves
1 finely sliced red spur chili
15g lime juice
2 tbsp all-purpose wheat flour
400g palm oil

Pat dry the fish fillet and dab the fish with lime juice. Cut the fish into 20g chunks • Lightly coat the fish with flour. In a frying pan, heat the oil over medium heat and when the oil is hot, fry the fish and remove from the pan when cooked to drain excess oil (do not fry until golden).

For ∎ serving of choo chee pla
5 pieces fried fish
150g choo chee curry base
Finely sliced kaffir lime leaves
Finely sliced red spur chilli

Place the fish in a pan and pour the curry base on top. Heat the ingredients over medium heat and lightly stir to coat the fish with the curry base. Continue to heat for 1-2 min • Plate the fish and sprinkle with sliced kaffir lime leaves and red chili.

Tips
Pan frying the fish helps remove the fishy smell and helps keep the fillet intact. Do not fry the fish until golden because the fillet will not be able to absorb the sauce.
Alternatively, this dish can also use prawns as main ingredient. Peel off the prawn shells, remove the heads, tails and dark veins across the backs but cutting along the curved back. Parboil the prawns in diluted coconut milk for pleasant aroma and tenderness of the meat. Moreover, other types of fish with chunky meat can be used for this dish such as red snapper, catfish or salmon.

Panang Gai

Chicken Panang Curry

The chicken in this dish must be tender and moist with curry base. The curry should have moderately thick consistency and the fat must not be separated. Panang curry should be dark red but not smooth texture due to roasted peanut mixture. The dish is fragrant from coriander seeds and has well-balanced flavors, a bit spicy but not sweet.

Panang curry base

100g panang curry paste (see page 153)
30g fish sauce
30g palm sugar
30g vegetable oil
250g thick coconut milk
500g thin coconut milk (250g thick
   coconut milk mixed with 250g water)

Heat the oil in a pan over medium heat, stir-fry the panang curry until fragrant then gradually add all coconut cream bit by bit and continue to stir-fry until the fat appears • Transfer the curry into a pot and slowly add the diluted coconut milk then adjust to low heat and continue to stir for 3 min. Season with fish sauce and sugar and stir-fry for another 3 min. Remove from heat and set aside in a bowl.

Other ingredients

300g chicken breast
250g thin coconut milk (60g thick
   coconut milk mixed with 190g water)
50g sweet basil leaves
4-5 kaffir lime leaves
1 finely sliced red spur chili

Cut the chicken breast across the grains into 10g pieces. Heat the diluted coconut milk over medium heat in a pot, as the coconut milk is hot, cook the chicken meat. Scoop out the chicken meat and set aside in a bowl.

For 1 serving of panang gai

10 pieces of chicken
120g panang curry base
1 shredded kaffir lime leaf (4 pieces)
6-7 sweet basil leaves
Finely sliced red spur chili

Add the chicken and panang curry base in a pan and stir well. Heat the mixture over low heat and as the mixture heats up add the kaffir lime leaf and sweet basil leaves and stir well. Adjust to medium heat and continue cooking for 15 seconds • Plate the curry and garnish with red chili.

Tips

The curry paste should be stir-fried in oil until cooked and fragrant before adding thick coconut milk, which should be adding gradually to prevent fat to separate and cause curdling.
If the curry paste is spicy, add 1 tbsp of roasted peanuts during stir-frying. Not suitable for people with peanut allergy (most ready-made panang curry paste consist of roasted peanuts).
For beef panang curry, top round steak is recommended for cooking. Cut the beef across the grains and simmer in thin coconut milk over low heat until tender.

Gaeng Massaman Gai

Chicken Massaman Curry

Ideally Massaman curry base should have thick consistency with dark curry color. Chicken meat should be tender and aromatic. This dish has well balanced flavors, not too hot or too sweet and salty. No presences of curdling in the curry sauce. Peanuts and potatoes are cooked and soft.

Massaman curry base

150g massaman curry paste (see page155)
30g vegetable oil
250g thick coconut milk
4-5 bay leaves
3 roasted cardamoms
1 roasted cinnamon stick (2 in. long)

Heat the vegetable oil in a pan over medium heat. As the oil is hot, stir-fry the curry paste until fragrant then gradually add all the thick coconut milk bit by bit. Add the bay leaves, roasted cardamoms and cinnamon and continue to stir-fry until fragrant. Set aside in a bowl.

Other ingredients

500g chicken thighs
60g palm oil for frying
625g thin coconut milk (315g thick
   coconut milk mixed with 310g water)
60g thick tamarind juice
50g palm sugar
65g fish sauce
65g bitter orange juice
3 potatoes (approx. 200g)
5 red onions (approx. 50g)
100g roasted peanuts

Wash the chicken thigh and pat it dry, then cut into cubes of 30g per piece • Heat the oil in a frying pan, as the oil is hot fry the chicken until the skin begins to cook. Set aside • Wash the potatoes. Boil the water and cook the potatoes. Soak the potatoes in cold water then peel and cut the potatoes into cubes of 15g per piece • Peel the onions and cut across in half horizontally. Parboil the onions in boiling water for 3 min. Scoop out to drain excess water. Boil the peanuts until they are soft and scoop out to drain excess water • Heat the thin coconut milk in a pot over medium heat. As the coconut milk is hot, cook the chicken, reduce to low heat and continue to cook until chicken is tender • Add the massaman curry base and stir well. Season with fish sauce, sugar, tamarind juice and bitter orange juice • Use a ladle to scoop out the chicken meat and set aside in a bowl. Continue to cook the curry over high heat for 20 min. Remove from the stove and pour the curry in a bowl.

Vinegar sauce

250g vinegar
100g sugar
5g ground sea salt
100g shallots
200g cucumber
1 small red spur chili

Mix the vinegar, sugar and salt together and place over low heat. Cook the ingredients until thick consistency and set aside in a bowl • Wash and peel the shallots and thinly slice vertically. Quarter the cucumber into long pieces. Thinly slice the red chili diagonally.
To serve In a small bowl, place 20g cucumber, 5g shallots, 3-4 pieces of sliced red chili and pour 20g of vinegar sauce over.

For 1 serving of gaeng massaman gai

4 pieces chicken
150 massaman curry base
2 pieces of potatoes
2 pieces of red onions
15g peanuts

Mix the chicken meat, potatoes, onions, peanuts and curry base in a pot. Heat for 2 min. over low heat. Serve warm with vinegar sauce.

Tips

Using overly high heat for coconut milk can cause curdling. Ready-made curry paste that has been stir-fried with oil may have excess oil on the surface, which can be scooped out before using it to stir-fry with coconut milk.

Simmering beef or chicken with the curry sauce can help the meat absorb the flavors from the sauce, then the meat can be set aside.

Bitter orange can be substituted with tangerine juice (green skin tengerine) by mixing 1 portion of lime juice with 2 portions of tangerine juice.

Gaeng Pet Gai

Chicken Red Curry

The curry sauce of this dish should be moderately thick with orange red color. The chicken meat is tender with over all well-balanced flavors. The curry is slightly less spicy than the Chicken Green Curry dish.

Curry base

100g red curry paste (see page 153)
30g vegetable oil
250g thick coconut milk
625g thin coconut milk (250g thick coconut milk mixed with 375g water)
30g fish sauce
25g palm sugar

Heat the vegetable oil in a pan over medium heat. Add the curry paste as the oil is hot and stir-fry until fragrant. Gradually add all the thick coconut milk bit by bit. Add the fish sauce and stir well • Transfer the curry into a pot. Add some thin coconut milk, sugar and stir well. Add the rest of the thin coconut milk and continue to cook over high heat for 1 min. Taste and season. Remove from heat and set aside in a bowl.

Other ingredients

300g chicken breasts
100g boiled pea eggplants (refer to cooking method in Gaeng Keaw Wan Gai recipe on page 62)
4-5 kaffir lime leaves
50g sweet basil leaves
1 red spur chili

Wash the chicken and pat dry. Cut the chicken across the grains into 5g pieces. Toss the chicken meat in 1 tsp of salt • Place the frying pan over high heat, as the pan is hot roast the chicken until cooked. Set aside.

For 1 serving of gaeng pet gai

16 pieces of chicken
190g curry base
1 shredded kaffir lime leaves (4 pieces)
10 pea eggplants
6-7 sweet basil leaves
2 pices of diagonally sliced red spur chili

Mix the chicken meat with curry base in a pot. Cook over medium heat and as the curry is hot, add kaffir lime leaves, sweet basil, pea eggplants and red chili. Stir well and continue to cook for 15 seconds. Ready to serve in a bowl.

Tips

Pan roasting the chicken helps enhance the pleasant aroma of the meat, keeps the meat tender and prevents foul smell when cooking it with curry base. It also tenderizes the chicken without having to simmer the meat over long period of time. Originally, this dish is called Red Curry due to the color of the curry paste.

Gaeng Garee Gai

Chicken Yellow Curry

This curry dish has yellow color with pleasant aroma and moderately thick consistency. The dominant flavor of this dish is salty without any hotness. Chicken meat is tender with sweetness from coconut milk. Potatoes are well cooked and soft.

Garee curry base
100g yellow curry paste (see page 155)
30g shallot oil
250g thick coconut milk
500g thin coconut milk (250g thick coconut milk mixed with 250g water)
5g ground sea salt

Heat the oil in a pan over medium heat. Add the curry paste as the oil is hot and stir-fry until fragrant. Gradually add all the thick coconut milk bit by bit. Add the sea salt and stir well • Transfer the curry into a pot and cook over medium heat. Gradually add all the diluted coconut milk bit by bit in order to prevent the fat curdling to the surface. Taste and season for a slightly salty flavor.

Other Ingredients
500g chicken breasts
50g fried shallots
250g vegetable oil
2 potatoes (150g each)

Cut the chicken across the grains into 10g pieces. Heat the oil in a pan over medium heat and as the oil heats up, cook the chicken meat until golden. Scoop out to drain excess oil • Boil some water in a pot and cook the potatoes for 30 min. Soak the potatoes in cold water immediately after cooking. As the potatoes cool down, peel and cut into cubes of 10g each.

Vinegar sauce
250g vinegar
100g sugar
5g ground sea salt
100g shallots
200g cucumbers
1 small red spur chili

Mix the vinegar, sugar and salt together and place over low heat. Cook the ingredients until thick consistency and set aside in a bowl • Wash and peel the shallots and thinly slice vertically. Quarter the cucumber into long pieces. Thinly slice the red chili diagonally.
To serve In a small bowl, place 20g cucumber, 5g shallots, 3-4 pieces of sliced red chili and pour 40g of vinegar sauce over.

For 1 serving of gaeng garee gai
8 pieces fried chicken
3 pieces potatoes
150g curry base
A pinch of fried shallots

Add the chicken, curry base and potatoes into pot to cook over medium heat. Stir the mixture well, place in a bowl and garnish with fried shallots. Serve with vinegar sauce on the side.

Tips
Pre-frying the chicken will keep the meat intact and prevent foul smell when cooking. The curry base should not be watery and clear. Stir-frying the curry paste with shallots oil will enhance the aroma of the dish. Vinegar sauce should have thick consistency for full flavors when pouring over the shallots and cucumber. Add sea salt to give the salty taste; do not use fish sauce.

Gaeng Nuea Prik Kee Noo

Beef Spicy Green Curry

The difference between beef curry and green curry is the coconut milk that is used to simmer the beef. The beef should be tender. The curry should have thick consistency, deep green color and more spicy than green curry with strong aroma from cumin and sweetness from coconut milk.

Curry base
120g green curry paste (see page 152)
5g roasted, crushed cumin
125g thick coconut milk
30g vegetable oil

Mix the curry paste and cumin together. Heat the oil in a pan over medium heat. Stir-fry the curry paste until fragrant and gradually add all the coconut milk bit by bit.

Other ingredients
1 kg top round or sirloin steaks
125g thick coconut milk
750g thin coconut milk (375g thick coconut milk mixed with 375g water)
45g fish sauce
15g palm sugar

Wash the steak and pat the meat dry. Cut the beef across the grains into 8g pieces • Heat the thin coconut milk over medium heat in a pot. Simmer the beef until tender • Add the curry base into the pot with simmering beef. Stir well. When the curry is hot, add fish sauce, sugar and thick coconut milk. Continue to cook for another 30 seconds. Taste and season for spicy, salty and a tinge of sweetness flavors • Use a ladle to scoop out the beef and set aside in separate bowl.

Other ingredients
50g bird's eye chilies
50g sweet basil leaves
4-5 kaffir lime leaves

For 1 serving of gaeng nuea prik kee noo
10 pieces of beef
125g curry base
6-7 bird's eye chilies
5-6 sweet basil leaves
1 shredded kaffir lime leaf (4 pieces)

Heat the curry base and beef in a pot. As the curry heats up, add the chilies and kaffir lime leaf and stir well. Continue to warm the curry then add the sweet basil leaves and keep them submerged. Ready to be served in a bowl.

Tips
The color of the curry should be consistent with the color of the beef. Simmering the beef with the curry base will help enhance the flavor of the beef and tenderize the meat. Recommended type of chili for this dish is bird's eye chilies with stems intact.

Hor Mok Pla Chon

Steamed Fish with Curry Paste in Banana Leaf Cups

Fish fillets in this dish should not have foul smell but aromatic and moist with curry sauce. The flavors should not be spicy or sweet from sugar, but with sweetness from coconut milk. The curried fish tops should be raised up from triangular fish stacks.

Main ingredients

1 kg snake-head fish fillets
125g thick coconut milk
625g thin coconut milk (375g thick coconut milk mixed with 250g water)
100g chili curry paste (see page 154)
10g finely pounded fingerroot
5g finely pounded kaffir lime zest
1 tsp ground pepper
2 chicken or duck eggs
50g fish sauce

Wash the fish fillet and pat dry. Slice into thin pieces weighing approximately 5g each and set aside • Pound the chili curry paste, fingerroot, kaffir lime zest and ground pepper together • Add the pounded mixture into a mixing bowl. Add the thick coconut milk, stir the mixture well, then add the fish fillets. Stir with a wooden spatula while gradually adding all the thin coconut milk bit by bit. Season with fish sauce and stir well. Add the eggs and stir the mixture until well blended.

Banana leaf cups

Fold 15 cups from banana leaves. Each cup with 4 corners and 4 in. diameter.

Other ingredients

½ cup thick coconut milk
1 tbsp rice flour
2 thinly sliced red spur chilies
6 thinly sliced kaffir lime leaves
200g sweet basil leaves

Mix the thick coconut milk and rice flour in a pot, place over medium heat and stir until the mixture thickens. (The mixture is used to pour over the fish curry) • Divide the sweet basil leaves into 15g portions and place each portion at the bottom of each cups • Add about 6-7 pieces of fish fillets in each cups, making a small triangle of fish stack. Pour the curry base into the cups • Arrange the cups into a steamer. Steam the curried fish for approximately 15 min. then remove from the steamer. Let cool and place in refrigerator.

For **1** serving of hor mok pla chon

2 cups of steamed curried fish
1 tbsp thick coconut milk
Thinly sliced red spur chili
Thinly sliced kaffir lime leaf

Boil the water in the steamer. Steam the curried fish for 10 seconds then remove from the steamer. Pour 1 tsp of thick coconut milk on top, garnish with red chili and kaffir lime leaf. Place the curry cups back in the steamer and continue to steam for 1 min. Serve warm.

Tips
Curry paste for this dish should not consist of spices, coriander seeds or cumin because they can cause bitter flavor.
Keep the quantity of fingerroot moderate and only use it for curried fish dish and not for other kinds of meat.
The thick coconut milk and curry paste should be well blended before adding the fish fillets.
Wooden spatula is suitable for mixing fish in order to keep the fillets intact.

STIR-FRIES

Pad Prik Khing Moo (Stir-Fried Pork with Red Curry Paste)
Pad Gaprao Gai (Stir-Fried Chicken with Holy Basil)
Pu Pad Prik Thai Dum (Stir-Fried Crab with Black Pepper)
Gai Pad Med Mamuang Himmapan (Stir-Fried Chicken with
   Cashew Nuts)
Pad Preaw Wan Moo (Stir-Fried Sweet and Sour Pork)
Pu Pad Pong Garee (Stir-Fried Crab in Curry Powder)

Pad Prik Khing Moo

Stir-Fried Pork with Red Curry Paste

Pork in this dish should be tender with aromatic fragrant of curry paste. The hot flavor of this dish is comparable to the hotness of ginger, hence the name "pad prik khing" (ginger in Thai is "khing"). The dish should be moist but not oily. Suitable for take away dish because it does not stale too quickly (without string beans). String beans bring balanced flavors to the dish and keep the spiciness balanced.

Seasoned red curry base
100g red curry paste (see page 153)
50g vegetable oil
80-90g palm sugar
60g fish sauce
30g water

Heat the vegetable oil over medium heat in a pan. As the oil is hot, add the curry paste and stir fry until fragrant. Reduce to low heat, add the fish sauce and palm sugar. Continue to stir fry • Add water and continue to stir-fry for 3 min. Taste and season for a slightly hot flavor with a tinge of sweetness and saltiness.

Other ingredients
300g pork loin
5 kaffir lime leaves
200g string beans

Boil 2 cups of water in a pot then add a pinch of salt. Boil the whole piece of pork loin and scoop out when cooked. Let the pork cool down before slicing into chunky pieces of 5g each • Boil 3 cups of water in a pot then add 1 tsp of salt. Boil the string beans for 1 min. and remove to soak in cold water immediately. As the string beans cool down, strain to drain excess water before cutting into 1-inch long pieces.

For 1 serving of pad prik khing moo
100g pork (20 pieces)
50-60g seasoned red curry base
6 pieces of string beans
15g water
½ tbsp finely sliced kaffir lime leaves

Mix the pork and seasoned red curry base in a pan then add water and mix well. Place the pan over medium heat and stir-fry until the mixture is hot. Adjust to high heat and continue to stir fry for 20 seconds, add the string beans, mix well and remove from heat. Garnish with kaffir lime leaves and ready to be served.

Tips
Pork or chicken for this dish should be boiled whole before slicing into small pieces in order to keep the meat tender. The meat should be sliced into thick pieces in accordance with the specified weight. Seasoned red curry base can be used to stir-fry with various kinds of meat such as crispy fried catfish, fish or mushrooms for vegetarians. Fish should be fried before stir-frying with the curry base, while mushrooms should be sliced into thin pieces before stir-frying.

Pad Gaprao Gai

Stir-Fried Chicken with Holy Basil

This dish does not use fresh chili due to its overly spicy taste. Pre-cooking the chicken or pork meat will prevent the foul smell from the meat, because the curry paste consists of galangal, garlic and coriander roots. Chicken and pork meat should be tender. The dominant flavor of this dish is spicy, followed by salty. There are 3 levels of hotness for this dish which are mild, medium and extra hot.

Seasoned holy basil mix

500g coarsely chopped chicken meat
80g holy basil curry paste (see page 156)
50g water
30g fish sauce
15g sugar
50g vegetable oil

Heat a frying pan over medium heat. Add the chicken (or pork) and fry until the meat is cooked. Set aside • Heat the oil in a frying pan over medium heat. As the oil heats up add the holy basil curry paste and stir-fry. Add the fish sauce, sugar and water. Reduce to low heat and continue to stir-fry until fragrant • Add the cooked chicken and increase to medium heat and stir well. Remove from heat and set aside.

Pad gaprao gai, medium hot

100g seasoned holy basil mix
5g holy basil curry paste (see page 156)
10-15 holy basil leaves
10g vegetable oil
30g water
5-6 crispy-fried holy basil leaves

Heat the vegetable oil over medium heat in a frying pan. As the oil heats up, add the holy basil curry paste and water then stir well • Add the seasoned holy basil mix and water and stir the mixture together. Add the holy basil leaves and stir well. Garnish with the crispy-fried holy basil leaves and ready to be served.
Pad gaprao gai, extra hot Add additional 10g of holy basil curry paste and follow the procedure for medium spicy flavor dish.

For **1** serving of pad gaprao gai, mild flavor

100g seasoned holy basil mix
10g vegetable oil
10-15 holy basil leaves
5-6 crispy fried holy basil leaves
30g water

Heat the vegetable oil over medium heat in a frying pan. Add the seasoned holy basil mix and water then stir well. Add the holy basil leaves and stir well. Serve in a plate and garnish with crispy fried holy basil leaves.

Tips

Chicken and pork meat should be coarsely chopped before stir-frying. Add the meat only when the pan is hot in order to keep the meat moist and tender without foul smell.
Palm oil should be used for deep-frying holy basil leaves. Add the leaves when the oil is hot and fry for 30-40 seconds. Strain the holy basil leaves immediately so they will not darken. Letting the leaves to crisp in the frying pan will burn the leaves.
Preparing the seasoned holy basil mix helps keep the taste of every dish consistent and enable adjustments to various level of hotness. The seasoned holy basil mix can be used to cook with other ingredients such as century eggs or stir fried with steamed rice.

Pu Pad Prik Thai Dum

Stir-Fried Crab with Black Pepper

The crab should be free from fishy smell and the meat should be loose from the shell. The sauce should have a well-balanced taste and not too thick. If the sauce becomes too thick, add clean water. The black pepper should be pounded coarsely and not finely.

Black pepper sauce

40g coarsely pounded roasted black
   peppercorns
30g finely chopped garlic
20g all-purpose wheat flour
60g sugar
100g fish sauce
50g vegetable oil
250g water

Heat the oil in a frying pan over medium heat. As the oil heats up, add the garlic and fry until fragrant. Add the flour and stir well. Add the black pepper and adjust to low heat • Add water, fish sauce and sugar. Stir until the mixture is well blended. Taste and season for a well-balanced taste with an obvious hotness. Continue to simmer the sauce until it thickens then remove from heat and set aside.

Other ingredients

3 sea crabs (400-500g each)
3 onions (80-100g each)
1 diagonally sliced red spur chili

Wash the crabs and steam over boiling water until cooked. Remove the abdomen and the shells and chop each crab into 4 sections • Peel the onions and cut into wedges of ½ cm thick.

For 1 serving of pu pad prik thai dum

4 pieces of crab (1 crab)
15g vegetable oil
40g wedged onions
60g black pepper sauce
2-3 diagonally sliced red spur chili

Heat the oil in a frying pan over medium heat. As the oil heats up, fry the onions until fragrant • Add the crab and the black pepper sauce, stir well and adjust to high heat for 30 seconds. Add the red chili and stir well. Ready to be served.

Tips

The coarsely pounded black peppers have different taste and texture than finely pound peppers when eaten. The hotness will vary with the various grain sizes of the pepper.
The sauce can be used to cook with other ingredients such as fish, prawns, mushrooms or tofu. Stir-frying the wheat flour will enhance the fragrance of the flour. Add water if the mixture becomes too dry.

Gai Pad Med Mamuang Himmapan

Stir-Fried Chicken with Cashew Nuts

Chicken in this dish should be tender, fragrant and tasty without foul smell and darkened color, cashew nuts crunchy, and onions cooked and sweet. The sauce should coat all the ingredients. The overall taste must not be too sweet or too oily. The stir-frying sauce base can be used to stir-fry with mushrooms or other vegetables.

Stir-frying sauce

30g finely chopped garlic
30g vegetable oil
50g sugar
50g light soy sauce
30g dark, sweet soy sauce
150g water
5g ground sea salt
5g all-purpose wheat flour

Heat the vegetable oil in a pan over medium heat. As the oil heats up, add the garlic and fry until fragrant. Add the flour and stir well then reduce to low heat • Add the ligh and dark soy sauce, stir well. Add water, sugar and sea salt then stir well. Taste and season for a well-balanced taste. The sauce should have slightly thick consistency.

Other ingredients

300g chicken breast, sliced across the grains into 5g pieces
10g light soy sauce
5g tapioca flour
15g vegetable oil
100g onions
6 stalks of spring onions, chopped into 1 inch-long pieces, using only the base of the stalk
150g fried cashew nuts
3 red spur chili, diagonally sliced
3 large dried chilies, cut across into 1 cm lengths

Marinate the chicken meat in soy sauce and flour for 20 minutes. Heat the oil in a frying pan and as the oil heats up add the marinated chicken meat and stir fry until the meat is cooked. Set aside • Peel the onions and slice into wedges of ½ cm thick.

For 1 serving of gai pad med mamuang himmapan

20 pieces of stir-fried chicken
4-5 fried dried chilies
50g wedged onions
50g cashew nuts
10g vegetable oil
4-5 pieces diagonally sliced red spur chili
15g chopped spring onions
50g stir-frying sauce

Heat the oil in a frying pan. As the oil heats up add the onions and stir-fry until fragrant • Add the chicken meat, cashew nuts and the sauce and stir-fry well. Increase to high heat then add the spring onions and the red spur chili and stir. Plate the mixture and garnish with dried chilies, ready to be served.

Tips
The stir-frying sauce is fragrant from the fried garlic. Frying the garlic until fragrant helps subdue the aroma of the soy sauces. The sauce should not be too thick. Add the cashew nuts last before stir-frying on high heat, if you prefer not to coat the nuts with the sauce. Green, red or yellow bell pepper may be added by cutting into small cubes of ½ inch and added to stir-fry with the onions.
Marinating the chicken with flour will help tenderize the meat. Light soy sauce should be used to marinate fish meat, and slightly coat the fish with wheat flour, then fry until golden.

Pad Preaw Wan Moo

Stir-Fried Sweet and Sour Pork

The dish should have pleasant aroma. The resulting sauce should have thick consistency and coats well on the ingredients. The pork is cooked and tender. The vegetables should not be over-cooked. The flavors are well balanced, not too sweet with sourness from tomatoes and pineapple.

Sweet and sour sauce
150g tomato sauce
60g vinegar
40g mild chili sauce
35g sugar
40g fish sauce
15g finely chopped garlic
170g vegetable oil

Heat the vegetable oil in a frying pan over medium heat. As the oil heats up, add the garlic and stir-fry until fragrant ● Add the tomato sauce, vinegar, sugar, fish sauce, chili sauce and water, then stir-fry well. Simmer over low heat for 10 more min. Taste and season for sour and salty taste.

Other Ingredients
100g pork loin, sliced across the grains
  into 5g pieces
150g cucumbers
100g onions
100g large tomatoes
100g sour pineapple

Boil 2 cups of water in a pot. Parboil the pork for 3 min, scoop out and set aside ● Cut both ends of the cucumber, halve the cucumber lengthways and slice diagonally into 1 in. thick pieces ● Cut the tomatoes into ½ in. wedges. Then cut the wedges in half ● Peel the onions and cut into 1 in. cubes ● Cut the pineapple into 5g cubes.

For 1 serving of pad preaw wan moo
10 pieces parboiled pork (50g)
5 pieces chopped cucumber (50g)
20g chopped onions
30g chopped tomatoes
5 pieces of chopped pineapple
10g vegetable oil
50g sweet and sour sauce

Heat the vegetable oil in a pan over medium heat. As the oil heats up, add the onions and stir-fry well. Add the pork and pineapple cubes, stir-fry well ● Add the sweet and sour sauce and cucumber, stir the mixture well. Add the tomatoes and increase to high heat. Stir-fry well.

Tips
Parboiling the pork makes the pork tender and removes the foul smell, while frying the pork in a pan will make the pork chewy.

If you are cooking with fish, the fish should be fried first. Lightly coat the fish with all-purpose wheat flour and fry until cooked, but not until golden since the fish will turn chewy. If you are cooking with prawns, parboil the prawns in boiling water instead of frying.

Green, red or yellow bell pepper can be added to enhance color, as well as to increase the nutrition of this dish.

No flour should be added to the sweet and sour sauce. Simmering the sauce will thicken the sauce.

Using the same brand of tomato sauce and chili sauce will keep the flavors consistent. Changing the brand will require tasting since the flavors may vary.

Pu Pad Pong Garee

Stir-Fried Crab in Curry Powder

The crab in this dish should be moist and easy to peel from the shells with good fragrance and no fishy smell. The overall taste should be well-balanced and not too sweet. The consistency of the sauce should be slightly thick.

Curry sauce

14g curry powder
20g finely chopped garlic
100g fish sauce
60g sugar
5g salt
10g ground pepper
500g un-sweetened condensed milk
50g vegetable oil

Heat the oil in a pan over medium heat. As the oil heats up, add the garlic and fry until fragrant. Add the curry powder and reduce to low heat and stir well. Add the fish sauce, sugar, salt and ground pepper. Stir well • Add the un-sweetened condensed milk and water and continue to heat for 2 min. Taste and season for a well-balance flavor. Continue to heat for another 2 min. until the sauce thickens. Set aside in a bowl.

Other ingredients

2 blue crabs (300-400g each)
100g onions, cut into wedges of ½ cm thick
1 red spur chili, sliced diagonally

Steam the crabs over high heat until cooked. Remove the abdomens and shells and chop each crab into 4 sections. Lightly crush the claws.

For 1 serving of pu pad pong garee

1 steamed blue crab
50g chopped onions
1 chicken egg, lightly whisked (optional)
5 pieces of diagonally sliced red spur chili
15g vegetable oil
50-60g curry sauce

Heat the vegetable oil in a pan. As the oil heats up, add the onions and stir-fry until fragrant • Add the crabs, curry sauce and eggs, and stir well together. Add the red spur chili and increase to high heat, continue to stir-fry for 20 seconds. Ready to be served.

Tips

The crabs should be steamed over boiling water until cooked before stir-fring. Cooked crab shells color turn red orange and does not have foul smell. Un-steamed crab meat is difficult to peel from the shells. Spring onions can be added as another ingredient, use the base part which are white and green in order to enhance the color of this dish.

If you are using prawns, the prawns should be parboiled until cooked to 70%. If you are using fish, the fish should be fried. Steaming the fish will cause the meat to be mushy with fishy smell. If you are using straw mushrooms or abalone mushrooms, they must be cut into thick pieces.

NOODLES AND RICE

Pad Thai Goong Sod (Stir-Fried Noodles with Prawns)
Mee Gati (Stir-Fried Noodles with Coconut Milk)
Sen Chan Pad Ganchiang Pu (Stir-Fried Rice Noodles
　　with Crab Legs)
Kao Klook Gapi (Stir-Fried Rice with Shrimp Paste)
Kao Pad Supparod (Fried Rice with Pineapple)

Pad Thai Goong Sod

Stir-Fried Noodles with Prawns

Soak flat rice noodles in water to soften them (warm water will break the noodles), drain the noodles and cover with thin white cloth. The noodles must be soft but does not cling together into clumps. The color of the noodles must be consistent and not too oily. The dish has pleasant aroma with well-balanced flavors.

Tamarind juice
1kg ripe tamarind
14 cups water (3½ kg)

Wash the tamarind and place in a bowl, add 1½ kg of water and soak for 10 min. Squeeze the tamarind and strain the juice with a strainer. Pour the juice in a pot • Add another 1½ kg of water in the bowl and squeeze the tamarind and strain more juice. Repeat the process again for the third time and strain the juice into the pot. Simmer the tamarind juice over low heat for 15 min. for pleasant aroma. Leave the juice to cool down, store in container and keep refrigerated.

Pad Thai sauce
260g tamarind juice
120g fish sauce
210g sugar

Mix all the ingredients together and stir until the sugar dissolves. Simmer over low heat for 30 min. until the sauce thickens. Set aside in a bowl.

For **1** serving of pad Thai goong sod
100g flat rice noodles (soaked in water until soften)
3 black tiger prawns (30g)
1 chicken egg
20g hard tofu, cut into 1 cm cubes
10g Chinese chives, cut into 1 in. pieces
50g bean sprouts, remove stringy tails
10g chopped salted pickled white radish
10g coarsely pounded roasted peanuts
5g finely chopped shallots
5g finely chopped garlic
30g vegetable oil
60-70g Pad Thai sauce
60g water

Peel the prawns, remove the heads and tails. Slice across the back to remove the veins. Parboil until cooked. Set aside • Heat 1 tbsp of vegetable oil in a pan over medium low heat. Add the garlic and shallots and stir-fry until fragrant. Then add the noodles and stir-fry well in the oil • Sprinkle 2-3 tbsp of water into the pan and stir-fry until the noodle softens. Set the noodles on one side of the pan, then add 2 tsp of oil, pickled white radish, tofu and prawns and stir-fry. Flip the noodles over the ingredients and stir-fry well together. Add the Pad Thai sauce and stir-fry the mixture well • Set the noodles on one side of the pan again. Increase the heat and add the rest of the oil. Add the egg and scramble the egg lightly. As the egg start to cook, flip the noodles over, add the bean sprouts and continue to stir-fry until the bean sprouts are cooked. Add the Chinese chives and peanuts and mix well • Plate the noodles, serve with 20g finely sliced banana blossoms (soaked in water mixed with lime juice to prevent discoloration), 5 gotu kola leaves, 20g bean sprouts, 3-4 stalks of Chinese chives and 1 lime wedge. Side condiments are chili powder and sugar.

Tips
Garlic and shallot make the oil fragrant, subduing the flour scent of the noodles.
Pad Thai sauce should use granulated sugar in order to be able to control the level of sweetness.
Pad Thai sauce can be stored in a container and refrigerated for 2-3 months. It can also be used to cook other dishes such as prawns in tamarind sauce, grilled prawns with tamarind sauce and fried shallots, or Thai papaya salad by mixing with finely pounded red chili and garlic.

Mee Gati

Stir-Fried Noodles with Coconut milk

The rice noodles (rice vermicelli) should be soft but do not break easily. The coconut milk sauce should have well- balanced flavors and faint pink in color from the prawn fats. The coconut milk should not curdle.

Coconut milk sauce

150g minced pork or chicken
1 river prawn (100g each), finely chopped
1 tsp vegetable oil
100g yellow tofu, cut into small cubes
1 tsp grounded dried chilies
80g fermented soya beans paste
70g sugar
70g thick tamarind juice
30g finely chopped shallots
750g coconut milk (500g thick coconut milk mixed with 250g water)

Wash the river prawn, remove the dark sac and squeeze out the prawn fats into a cup. Peel the prawn, remove the head and tail, cut into small pieces and finely chop the prawn meat • Heat the oil in a pan over low heat. As the oil heats up, stir-fry the prawn fats until fragrant and set aside in a bowl • Mix the minced pork and prawn meat together • Heat the coconut milk in a pan over medium heat. As the oil begins to rise on the surface, add the shallots and fry until fragrant • Add the pork, prawns, soya bean paste, sugar, tamarind juice, tofu, and ground chilies then mix well. Add the prawn fats and stir. Taste to season for well-balanced flavors. Set aside in a bowl.

For 1 serving of mee gati

120g rice noodles, soaked in water to soften
10g Chinese chives, cut into 1 in. pieces
40g bean sprouts, stringy tails removed
60g coconut milk sauce
20g coconut milk sauce for topping
10g shredded fried eggs (refer to stir-fried rice with shrimp paste recipe)
Some thinly sliced red spur chilies
3 stalks of Chinese chives

Heat the pan over medium heat. As the pan heats up add the coconut milk sauce and rice noodles and stir-fry until the noodles soften. Add the bean sprouts and Chinese chives. Add more water if the mixture becomes too dry so the noodles are soft and moist • Plate the stir-fried noodles and garnish with coconut milk sauce on top with shredded fried eggs and thinly slice red chilies • Serve with 20g finely sliced banana blossom (soaked in water mixed with lime juice to prevent discoloration), 5 gotu kola leaves, 20g bean sprouts, 3-4 stalks of Chinese chives, 1 lime wedge, and chili powder.

Tips

The rice noodle should be soaked moderately in water. Do not leave the noodles in water too long as it may cause the noodles to break during the cooking process. After soaking until soften, drain the excess water and cover the noodles with thin white cloth.
If the sauce becomes too dry, add more thin coconut milk.
Use organic femented soya bean paste as it is not overly salty and has pleasant smell.

Sen Chan Pad Ganchiang Pu

Stir-Fried Rice Noodles with Crab legs

The flat rice noodles in this dish should be soft but do not break easily and does not cling together in clumps. The noodles are slightly red from chilies. Well prepared sauce has pleasant aroma and is not to dry or too soggy.

Stir-fry sauce

15g large dried chilies
100g palm sugar
40g fish sauce
50g tamarind juice
60g water
5g salt
15g sliced shallots
15g sliced garlic
30g vegetable oil

Remove the seeds from the dried chilies and soak the chilies in water until soften. Squeeze excess water out and finely slice the chilies. Pound the chilies with salt then add shallots and garlic. Pound the mixture well together • Heat the oil in a pan over medium heat. Add the mixture and stir-fry until fragrant, then reduce to low heat. Add water and season with fish sauce, sugar and tamarind juice then stir well. Simmer until the sauce thickens. Taste for well-balanced flavors of sour, salty, sweet and spicy.

For 1 serving of sen chan pad ganchiang pu

100g Chan noodles (flat rice noodles), soaked in water until softened
80g steamed crab legs
20g vegetable oil
60g stir-fry sauce
25g bean sprouts, stringy tails removed
20g Chinese chives, cut into 1 in. pieces
30g water

Heat the oil in a pan over medium heat. As the oil heats up, add the noodles and stir-fry to coat the noodle with the oil. Add water and stir-fry until the noodles soften. Reduce to low heat • Add the sauce and crab legs and stir-fry well. Scoop out the crab leg and set aside. Increase to high heat then add the bean sprouts and stir-fry until cooked. Add the Chinese chives and stir-fry quickly. As the mixture dries up, remove from heat. Plate the noodles with crab legs on the top • Serve with bean sprouts, Chinese chives and 1 lime wedge.

Tips

Stir-frying the noodles with the oil first prevents the noodle to cling together into clumps. Adding water while stir-frying soften the noodles before adding the sauce. If you are cooking with prawns, the prawns should be cooked first (similar to pad Thai with prawns preparation), in order to prevent fishy smell and enhance fragrance. Stir-frying the pounded mixture enhances the aroma of the sauce. Taste the sauce before storing in container due to the inconsistency of the tamarind sour flavor.

Kao Klook Gapi

Stir-Fried Rice with Shrimp Paste

The rice should be soft and all coated with the shrimp paste sauce, with pleasant aroma, not too dry and not soggy with well-balanced flavors. The shrimp paste should be stir-fried over low heat since high heat will cause the paste to burn and taste bitter. Recommended technique to cook rice is to use jasmine rice and drain the rice with water once before mixing the rice with 1 tbsp of vegetable oil before adding the water for cooking. With this procedure, the rice will not cling in clumps when cooked.

Shrimp paste sauce
50g shrimp paste
200g water
20g powdered dried shrimps
30g sugar
30g lime juice
20g minced garlic
40g vegetable oil

Other ingredients
300g cooked rice
100g thinly sliced pork tenderloin
50g shallots
100g green mango
2 tsp vegetable oil
1 lime
1 egg, whisked
1 red spur chili
2 cucumbers

Braised Eggs
20 hard-boiled eggs, shells remove
20g finely pounded coriander roots
20g finely pounded garlic
1 tsp ground pepper
100g palm sugar
60g light soy sauce
15g dark soy sauce
1,500g water (6 cups)
1 roasted cinnamon stick (2 in. long)
3 roasted star anise
30g vegetable oil

Heat the oil in a pan over medium heat. As the oil heats up, add the garlic and stir-fry until fragrant • Separate 30g of water to mix with the shrimp paste then add to a pan over low heat. Add the rest of the water and stir well • Add sugar, lime juice, and powdered dried shrimps. Taste and season for well-balanced flavors. Add more sugar if the mixture is too salty. Continue to heat until the sauce thickens and stick to the spatula. Remove from heat and set aside in a bowl.

Shredded fried eggs - Heat the oil in a pan over medium heat. As the oil heats up add the whisked eggs and roll the pan around to form thin sheet of cooked egg. Once the egg is cooked, remove from the pan. Roll the eggs and thinly slice into small shreds • Heat a pan over medium heat. As the pan heats up, stir-fry the pork until cooked and set aside Peel and wash the shallots. Thinly slice the shallots vertically • Peel the green mango and slice into thin sheets. Stack the mango sheets and slice into long strands.

Pound the coriander roots, garlic and ground pepper together • Heat the oil in a pan over medium heat. As the oil heats up, stir-fry the pounded mixture until fragrant then reduce to low heat. Add the light soy sauce, dark soy sauce and palm sugar and stir well. Add ½ cup of water and stir the mixture well • Add the eggs in a pan, use a spatula to coat the eggs with the mixture. Scoop out the eggs and transfer into a pot. Add water and cook over low heat. Add the star anise pods and cinnamon stick and continue to simmer until the mixture seeps into the eggs • Leave the eggs to cool and keep the eggs and sauce in a container and refrigerated. Only take the egg to use for making kao klook gapi.

For 1 serving of kao klook gapi

150g cooked rice
50g shrimp paste sauce
25g cooked pork
20g sliced shallots
25g sliced green mango
10g shredded eggs
1 cucumber, quartered and cut in halves
1 braised egg, quartered
30g sliced green mango as side dish
½ lime
Thinly sliced red spur chili

Add the sauce, pork and rice into a pan. Toss all the ingredients well together so the sauce coats all the rice • Place the pan over medium heat and stir-fry the rice. Reduce to low heat then add the sliced shallots and stir-fry well. Remove from heat. Add the sliced green mango and mix well. Plate the mixture and sprinkle shredded eggs and red chili on top. Serve with cucumber, green mango, lime, and braised egg.

Tips

Green mango and shallots in the dish enhance the flavors of this dish. Braised eggs is better than sweet stir-fried pork in dark soy sauce in completing the overall taste.

This dish is high in calcium because it contains shrimp paste, which has 1,554 mg of calcium per 100g, 1 egg contains 61 mg of calcium, and dried shrimp is also high in calcium.

Kao Pad Supparod

Fried Rice with Pineapple

Tip in cooking good rice lies in the removal of imperfect grains before cooking. The fried rice should be soft with strong pineapple smell from the pineapple flesh and pineapple juice; the rice is not too dry or too soggy. The overall flavor is well-balanced. Rice grains must be well intact. Pineapple selected for this dish must not be too ripe due to better taste and color. The pineapple must be stir-fried until fragrant before adding the rice. Serving the fried rice in a pineapple bowl enhances the pleasant fragrant of the fried rice, and pineapple also increases the nutritional value of the dish.

Fried rice
250g cooked rice
5g sugar
10g fish sauce
¼ tsp ground pepper
30g vegetable oil

Heat the oil in a pan over medium heat. As the oil heats up add the cooked rice and season with fish sauce, sugar and ground pepper. Stir-fry well and set aside in a plate.

Other ingredients
½ kg white prawns (size 50/60)
150g chicken breasts
50g pineapple, cut into cubes
1 onion (100g)
2 bell pepper, red and green
1 pineapple, with crown and stem
1 whisked egg and 1 tsp vegetable oil
   for egg strands (refer to kao klook gapi
   recipe)

Peel the prawns, remove the heads and tails. Remove the veins then cut into small pieces. Toss the prawn meat with ¼ tsp of fish sauce. Heat the pan and cook the prawns. Set aside • Slice the chicken breasts into small pieces of 3g each. Toss the meat with ¼ tsp of fish sauce. Cook the chicken meat. Set aside • Cut the red and green spur chilies and onions into big cubes of 1½ cm • Wash the pineapple to make a bowl. Lay the pineapple on its side. Split the pineapple vertically into 2 sections, making a bowl and a lid. The bottom of the pineapple bowl still has crown attached, so the lid section is slightly smaller. From the bottom section, scoop out all pineapple flesh and core, then cut into small cubes of ½ inch. Squeeze out the pineapple juice from the rest of the flesh. Scoop out all the flesh from the pineapple lid.

For 1 serving of kao pad supparod
250g fried rice
100g cooked chicken
50g cooked prawns
50g pineapple flesh
10g vegetable oil
20g onions
20g red and green bell pepper (10g each)
60g pineapple juice
Egg strands for garnish

Heat the oil in a pan over medium heat. As the oil heats up, add the onions and stir-fry then add the pineapple to stir-fry for 10 seconds until fragrant • Add the rice, chicken and prawns and stir-fry well together. Add the pineapple juice and mix well. Add the bell pepper, increase to high heat and continue to stir-fry for 30 seconds • Place the fried rice in the prepared pineapple bowl, then cover the bowl with aluminum foil. Bake the pineapple bowl in the oven at low heat for 10 minutes until hot and fragrant. Remove from the oven and garnish with egg strands on top to serve. The fried rice can also be served on a plate.

Tips

For cooked rice that is soft with perfect grains, wash and drain the rice once before cooking. Add 1 tbsp of vegetable oil for 1 kg of rice and stir well before adding water for cooking.

Egg strands should be made from slight thick sheet of cooked egg, in order for the egg to be soft and prevent the sheet from sticking to a pan. They should not be sliced too long prior to use, since the egg strands will harden.

APPETIZERS

Kao Hor Song Kreuang (Deep-Fried Rice Samosas)
Satay Rai Mai (Skewerless Satays)
Tod Mun Pla Grai (Thai Fish Cakes)
Gai Hor Bai Toey (Chicken Wrapped in Pandan Leaves)
Tod Mun Goong (Deep-Fried Shrimp Patties)
Poh Pia Tod (Deep-Fried Spring Rolls)
Kanom Pang Na Goong (Deep-Fried Shrimp Canapés)
Toong Tong (Deep-Fried Golden Pouches)

Kao Hor Song Krueang

Deep-Fried Rice Samosas

The samosas should be crispy but not oily and golden in color. The overall taste should well-balanced. The dipping sauce should be thick and stick well to the rice samosas when dipped. The seams where the flour glue was applied should not be burnt from over frying.

Dipping sauce
30g finely chopped deseeded red spur chilies
120g vinegar
10g ground sea salt
100g sugar

Pound the chilies and sea salt finely together. Mix the pounded mixture with vinegar and sugar and stir until the sugar dissolves. Simmer over low heat until the sauce thickens then remove from heat and set aside.

Ingredients
80g white prawns
50g minced pork
10g finely chopped coriander roots
25g finely chopped garlic
1 tsp ground pepper
¼ tsp ground sea salt
150g cooked rice
30g fish sauce
1 chicken egg, whisked
80g bean sprouts, stringy tails removed
80g grated carrots
30g vegetable oil for stir-frying
500g palm oil for deep-frying
30 spring roll sheets (6-inch diameter)
Flour glue (3 tbsp all-purpose wheat flour mixed with 2-3 tbsp water)

Wash the prawns. Peel off the shells, remove heads, tails and dark veins. Cut into small pieces and finely chop prawn meat to 50g • Pound the coriander roots, garlic, salt, and pepper together into a fine paste. Mix the minced pork and prawn meat together. Add the mixture to the mortar and pound with the paste • Gradually add the cooked rice while pounding lightly, alternating with adding the fish sauce bit by bit. As the rice grains break add the bean sprouts and carrots and continue to pound lightly. Add the whisked egg and mix well together • Heat the vegetable oil over medium heat. As the oil heats up, add the mixture and stir-fry until the mixture is cooked and dried up. Set aside in a bowl.

Filling
Cut the spring roll sheets into two identical size. Placing the uneven surface outward and the smooth surface inward and fold the sheet into triangular cone shape. Apply the flour glue at the seam and fill 1½-2 tsp of fried rice inside. Apply the flour glue on top of the cone and seal close tightly • Heat the palm oil in a pan over medium heat. As the oil is hot, add approximately 15 rice samosas into the oil to deep fry, flip the samosas back and forth for 2 minutes. Do not fry until golden. Scoop out and drain excess oil. (First deep-frying is for the samosas to start to crisp). Leave to cool and stack the samosas in a container, separating each layer with grease paper. Close the lid and keep refrigerated.

For 1 serving of kao hor song krueang
6 pre-fried rice samosas
500g palm oil for deep-frying
45g dipping sauce

Heat the oil in a pan over high heat. As the oil heats up reduce to medium heat. Deep-fry the rice samosas by flipping back and forth for 3-4 minutes until golden. Remove from the pan and drain excess oil • Serve on a plate with dipping sauce on the side.

Tips

Flour glue is made from all-purpose wheat flour mixed with water to a moderately thick consistency. The flour glue is used to seal the opening of the samosas. Deep-frying once will not burn the flour glue at the seams. However, stirring the flour glue mixture over the heat before applying will cause the seams to burn because the flour will be cooked twice.

Deep-frying should be done twice in palm oil. The purpose of first deep-frying is to precook the spring roll sheets. The second deep frying makes the rice samosas golden in color. Deep-frying the rice samosas twice will make the samosas crispy and not oily.

Satay Rai Mai

Skewerless Satays

Pork and chicken satays should be tender and aromatic, similar to being grilled over charcoal. The satay sauce should have thick consistency, pleasant smell, not sweet and have well-balanced flavors. Moreover, no excess oil on the surface. The cucumber in the vinegar sauce should be crisp and tasty.

Satay sauce

50g chili paste
65g finely grounded rosted peanuts
750g thin coconut milk (375g thick
  coconut milk mixed with 375g water)
2 tsp ground roasted coriander seeds
1 tsp ground roasted cumin seeds
1 tbsp ground sea salt (15g)
150g palm sugar
110g tamarind juice
40g oil for stir-frying

Mix the chili paste, coriander seeds and cumin seeds together. Heat the oil in a pan over medium heat. As the oil heats up, add the mixture and stir-fry until fragrant • Gradually add all the coconut milk bit by bit while stirring. Add the palm sugar and tamarind juice, mix well together. Reduce to low heat, then add the peanuts. Simmer until the sauce thickens. Taste and season for well-balanced flavors. Avoid using high heat to prevent oil rising to the surface. Remove from the heat. Leave to cool, place in a bowl then keep refrigerated.

Vinegar sauce

250g vinegar
200g sugar
15g ground sea salt
60g water

Mix the vinegar, sugar, salt and water together. Stir well until the sugar dissolves. Simmer the sauce over low heat until it thickens. Remove from the heat.

Vegetables

6 cucumbers
5 shallots
2 red spur chilies

Other Ingredients

500g pork loin or thighs
500g chicken breasts
20g finely chopped lemongrass
10g finely chopped galangal
2 tsp ground roasted coriander seeds
1 tsp ground roasted cumin seeds
1 tbsp powdered turmeric
250g thick coconut milk
10 ground sea salt
20g sugar
250g thin coconut milk to sprinkle
  over satays (125g thick coconut milk
  mixed with 125g water)

Slice the pork and chicken across the grain, 1 in. wide and 3 in. thick, weighin about 12g per piece • Pound the lemongrass and galangal together into a fine paste. Add the cumin seeds and coriander seeds and salt, then finely pound the mixture well • Mix the paste with coconut milk in a mixing bowl, add the turmeric and stir well. Use this as satay marinate sauce • Divide the marinate sauce into 2 portions. Separately knead the pork and chicken meat until tender. Add each portion to the pork and chicken meat (separately). Lightly mix the meat and the marinate sauce together. Marinate for 1 hour • Sprinkle coconut milk on two baking trays. Arrange the pork and chicken meat on separate trays then sprinkle more coconut milk over the meat. Roast in the oven, set to 350 Fahrenheit for 5 min. Remove from the oven, as the meat cool down, place in a container, lid closed and keep refrigerated.

For 1 serving of satay rai mai

5 pork satays
5 chicken satays
50g thin coconut milk to sprinkle
40g satay sauce
20g vinegar sauce
50g cucumber, vertically quartered then
sliced into ¼ cm-thick pieces
2 shallots, thinly sliced
4-5 pieces of sliced red spur chili

Sprinkle coconut milk on a grilling pan, then arrange the skewers of satay on the pan. Heat the pan over medium high heat and sprinkle the coconut milk during grilling. As the meat is cooked and becomes aromatic, flip the meat to cook on both sides with evenly golden color • Place the cucumber, shallots and chili in a small bowl then pour the vinegar sauce over the vegetables • Arrange the cooked satays on a plate, serve with satay sauce and cucumber salad in vinegar sauce on the side.

Tips

The pork and chicken meat should be kneaded until tender (or pounded with a meat pounder) in order for the satay marinate sauce to absorb well. The turmeric should be added last because adding together with other ingredients will cause the mortar to have yellow stain, which is difficult to clean.

Pre-grilling the pork and chicken until almost cooked and keeping them refrigerated will enable longer storage time. If the meat is refrigerated without being pre-grilled, the meat will turn sour and lack aromatic smell. Pre-grilling can also save time before serving.

Thick cast-iron pan is recommended. Sprinkling the coconut milk while grilling will make the satay tender and aromatic. Only slice the cucumbers before serving, instead of using stored vegetables. The cucumbers will be fresh and crisp.

Tod Mun Pla Grai

Thai Fish Cakes

The fish cakes should be moderately sticky and have pleasant aroma. The pieces should not be too oily or wrinkly in texture and free from fishy smell. The cucumber salad in vinegar sauce for dipping should have well-balanced flavors. The cucumber should be crisp.

Dipping Sauce

125g vinegar
5 ground sea salt
100g sugar
50g coarsely pound roasted peanuts
200g cucumber, vertically halved and sliced into ½ cm thick pieces (If long cucumber is used, its skin should be peeled off and seeds removed.)
2 red spur chilies, sliced into ½ cm thick pieces

Mix the sugar, vinegar, and salt together and stir until all sugar dissolves. Simmer over low heat to enhance the flavors until the sauce thickens. This is called "seasoned vinegar sauce."

Ingredients

500g clown knifefish meat
100g chili curry paste
10g finely pound coriander roots
10g finely pound garlic
100g finely sliced winged beans
5g ground sea salt
30g water
1 tbsp finely sliced kaffir lime leaves

Mix the salt and water together. The salted water is used to sprinkle over the fish meat during kneading process to make the fish cake mixture turn sticky more quickly • Mix the chili paste, garlic and coriander roots together. Remove all the bones from the fish and add the paste to the fish meat. Knead the mixture while gradually sprinkle salted water over until the fish patty becomes moderately sticky • Sprinkle the kaffir lime leaves and winged beans and continue to knead the mixture. Mold the mixture into round patties weighing about 35g each. Arrange the fish cakes in a lightly oiled tray. Steam the fish cakes over boiling water for 5 min. until 70% cooked. Remove from heat and leave to cool. Stack the fish cakes in a container in layers, separating each layer with a plastic sheet to avoid the fish cakes sticking to each other. Cover and keep refrigerated.

For 1 serving of tod mun pla grai

5 pieces of fish cakes
250g palm oil for deep-frying
4-5 slices of red spur chili
1 tbsp roasted peanuts
40g seasoned vinegar sauce
30g cucumber

Heat the oil in a pan over medium heat. As the oil heats up, deep-fry the fish cakes. The fish cakes will float up to the surface when cooked, scoop out to drain excess oil. Plate the fish cakes and serve with dipping sauce • To prepare dipping sauce, add the cucumber and red chili in a small bowl. Pour the seasoned vinegar over the vegetables and top with the roasted peanuts.

Tips
Fish cakes should not contain eggs because they will bloat up immediately after deep-frying but will wrinkle after they cool down. Adding the coriander roots and garlic in the chili paste will enhance the aroma of the fish cakes.
Cooking the fish cakes to 70% will help retain the sticky consistency of the fish meat and enhance the pleasant aroma of the spices. If the fish cakes are not pre-cooked, they will not have desired consistency after deep-frying.

Gai Hor Bai Toey

Chicken Wrapped in Pandan Leaves

The chicken should be tender, moist, and tasty with pleasant aroma. The dipping sauce should not have pungent smell of the soy sauce.

Dipping sauce
200g sugar
100 dark sweet soy sauce
125g water
20g ground sea salt
25g lightly pound roasted white sesame
   seeds

Mix the sugar and water together. Place the mixture over medium heat and as the mixture boils, add the dark sweet soy sauce and salt. Continue to boil for 1 more min. and stir until the mixture thickens. Remove from the heat and set aside in a bowl.

Ingredients
1kg chicken breasts
15g finely chopped coriander roots
5g ground pepper
2 tbsp finely chopped garlic (30g)
30g fish sauce
30g light soy sauce
15g Chinese vinegar
125g thick coconut milk
5g ground sea salt
10g sugar
50 large pandan leaves for wrapping

Wash the chicken and slice the meat across the grains to 20g pieces • Pound the coriander roots, garlic, and pepper together. Add the fish sauce, light soy sauce, Chinese vinegar, coconut milk, salt and sugar. Stir until the mixture is all blended well together. Use this mixture as marinate sauce • Pour the mixture on the chicken in a bowl, mix well and marinate for 1 hour • Wrapping: Wash and wipe the pandan leaves clean and dry. Fold a pandan leaf into a loose knot and place 1 piece of marinated chicken inside. Tighten the knot on the chicken and insert the tips properly. The chicken meat must be fully covered with the pandan leaves, otherwise the exposed chicken meat will burn during deep-frying. Steam the wrapped chicken over boiling water. Store the wrapped chicken in a closed container and keep refrigerated.

For 1 serving of gai hor bai toey
5 pieces of chicken in pandan leaves
250g palm oil for deep-frying
30g dipping sauce
¼ tsp roasted white sesame seeds

Heat the oil in a deep-frying pan over medium heat. As the oil heats up, deep-fry the chicken in pandan leaves until the leaves turn greenish brown (not burnt). Scoop out from the pan and drain excess oil. Serve with the dipping sauce sprinkled with sesame.

Tips
Preparing the marinate sauce separately before adding to the chicken will keep the flavors of the chikcen meat balanced with consistent aroma. This procedure is better than adding the herbs and seasoning directly to the chicken meat.
The coconut milk helps tenderize the chicken. Fish with chunky meat can be used as an alternative to chicken meat.

Tod Mun Goong

Deep-Fried Shrimp Patties

The shrimp patties should be tender, not soggy and not too chewy. The smell of the patties should be pleasant, the bread crumbs not too thick nor oily. The prune sauce should have well-balanced flavors with nice prune aroma and smooth texture.

Prune sauce

80g prunes, deseeded
120g water
60g orange juice
40g lime juice
½g ground sea salt
30g brown sugar
15g vinegar
15g all-purpose wheat flour

Bring the water to a boil over medium heat. Add the prunes, reduce to low heat and boil until the prunes are cooked. Mash the prunes into fine paste and transfer into another pot • Mix a bit of water and flour together. Add the sugar, salt, orange juice, venegar and lime juice, then stir well. Add the mixture into the pot with the mashed prunes. Simmer the mixture over low heat and stir well until the sauce thickens. Remove from the heat.

Other ingredients

800g white prawns
50g hard pork fat, chopped into small pieces
7 peppercorns
15g finely chopped coriander roots
20g finely chopped garlic
½ tsp ground sea salt
25g fish sauce
1 chicken egg
250g bread crumbs

Wash the prawns, peel the shells, and remove the heads and tails. Slit across the back to remove dark veins. Finely chop 500g of prawn meat and mash the prawns with chopped pork fat in a mixing bowl • Pound the coriander roots, garlic, pepper and salt together. Add the pounded mixture in the mixing bowl with the fish sauce. Mix the prawns and herbs well together by kneading until the mixture becomes sticky. Add the egg and knead well • Mold the mixture into round patties weighing about 35g each. Then roll the patties in bread crumbs. Arrange the patties in the steamer and steam over boiling water until they are 50% cooked. This helps retain the prawns' texture when deep-frying. Remove the patties from the steamer and leave to cool. Store in a container by using plastic sheets to separate each layers of the patties. Cover and keep refrigerated.

For 1 serving of tod mun goong

4 shrimp patties
30g all-purpose wheat flour
1 chicken egg, whisked
½ cup bread crumbs
250g palm oil for deep-frying
40g prune sauce

Heat the oil in a pan over medium heat. As the oil heats up, roll the patties in the flour lightly, dip in the egg and then roll in the bread crumbs. Deep fry the shrimp patties in the pan until golden. Scoop out from the pan and drain excess oil. Serve with the prune sauce on the side. (Prune sauce enhances the taste of the shrimp patties and also add nutritional value to the dish.)

Tips

The prawns must be patted dry before chopping into small pieces for mashing with pork fat. Adding pork fat with the prawn meat will help tenderize the patties. Using lard will cause the shrimp patties to have runny texture.

Poh Pia Tod

Deep-Fried Spring Rolls

The spring rolls should be golden, crispy but not oily. The dipping sauce should be thick and coat well on the spring rolls. Edges of the spring rolls should not be burnt from frying.

Dipping sauce
125g vinegar
100g sugar
15g ground sea salt
10g finely chopped red spur chili
15g finely chopped garlic
10g finely chopped coriander roots
1 tsp tapioca flour

Finely pound the chili, coriander roots, salt, and garlic together • Add sugar and vinegar into the mixture and mix well. Add the tapioca flour and stir until the flour dissolves. Simmer the mixture over low heat until the sauce thickens. Remove from the heat and set aside in a bowl.

Spring roll filling
25g vermicelli
100g minced pork
50g finely sliced ear mushrooms
7 peppercorns
25g finely chopped garlic
10g ground sea salt
15g finely chopped coriander roots
30g fish sauce
15g finely chopped garlic for frying
150g shredded cabbage
100g bean sprouts, stringy tails removed
100g grated carrots
40g oil for stir-frying

Soak the vermicelli in water until it softens. Drain and cut into short pieces • Pound the pepper, garlic, coriander roots, and salt together. Add the fish sauce and stir the mixture well • Heat the oil in a pan over medium heat. As the oil heats up, add the garlic and fry until fragrant. Add the pounded mixture and continue to stir-fry until fragrant. Add the minced pork, ear mushrooms, and vermicelli and stir-fry until the ingredients begin to cook then add the cabbage, bean sprouts and carrots. Stir-fry until all ingredients are cooked and dry. Remove from the heat and set aside.

Other ingredients
300g spring roll sheets, 6 in. diameter
30g all-purpose wheat flour
50g water
1,000g palm oil for deep-frying

Wrapping
Mix the wheat flour with water to make flour glue • Spread the spring roll sheets on a cutting board, smooth side upwards, in order for the spring rolls to have crispy and fluffy texture after deep-frying. Add 20g of filling on each sheet. Fold the edges, roll the sheet tightly over the filling and apply flour glue to seal the roll • Preheat the oil in a pan over medium heat. Fry the spring rolls in the hot oil and flip the rolls from side to side for 2 min. As the spring roll sheets begin to cook, scoop out and leave to drain excess oil. As the spring rolls cool down, store in a container by stacking the rolls into layers, separating each layer with grease paper. Cover and keep refrigerated.

For **1** serving of poh pia tod
6 spring rolls
500g palm oil for deep-frying
30g dipping sauce

Preheat the oil in a frying pan over high heat. As the oil heats up, add the spring rolls and deep-fry for 3-4 min. until golden. Scoop out with a strainer and leave to drain excess oil. Ready to be served with the dipping sauce on the side.

Tips

Frying the spring rolls twice enhances the crispiness and prevents oil to absorb into the rolls. Spring rolls that are wrapped and stored without pre-frying will be soggy and not crispy after deep-frying.

Using fresh flour glue to seal the edges of the spring rolls prevents the edges from burning. However, using cooked flour glue will cause the edges to burn due to double-frying.

Kanom Pang Na Goong

Deep-Fried Shrimps Canapés

The canapés should not be oily, the bread is evenly golden after deep-frying. The flavors are well-balanced. The dipping sauce should be thick and coats well on the canapés when dipping. The flavors of the dipping sauce should be sour with sweet twist and not spicy. Orange zest jam in the dipping sauce enhances the flavors of the sauce with an orange zest aroma twist and touch of bitterness.

Dipping sauce

30g finely chopped red spur chilies,
   seeds removed
120g orange zest jam
150g vinegar
10g ground sea salt
10g finely pounded coriander roots
20g finely pounded garlic

Pound the chili, coriander roots, and garlic together • Add the rest of the ingredients to the mixture. Heat the mixture over medium heat and stir well. Taste and season for well-balanced flavors. Simmer until the sauce thickens then remove from the heat. Set aside.

Shrimp canapé

18 slices of sandwich bread
500g white prawns
200g pork loin
20g garlic
15g finely chopped coriander roots
5 peppercorns
5g ground sea salt
20g fish sauce
1,000g vegetable oil

Wash the pork and mince well. Peel the prawns, remove heads and tails. Cut across the back to remove dark veins. Chop the prawn meat finely. Mix the pork and prawns together • Pound the garlic, coriander roots, pepper and salt together well. Add the pork and prawn meat to the mixture and season with fish sauce. Continue to pound the mixture lightly until the topping is well blended. Adding the pork into the prawn meat helps tenderize and smoothen the texture of the meat for the topping. • Quarter the sandwich bread into 4 even squares. Air-dry the bread • Spoon about 1 tbsp of the topping onto the bread to make a canapé. Smoothen the top • Arrange all the canapés on a baking tray and bake in the oven in 350° F heat for 3 min. until the canapés begin to cook. Remove the canapés from the heat and leave to cool. Store the canapés in a container in layers, separating each layer with plastic sheets. Cover and keep refrigerated.

For 1 serving of kanom pang na goong

8 shrimp canapés
1 chicken egg, whisked
500g palm oil for deep-frying
30g dipping sauce
Coriander leaves
Finely sliced red spur chili

Preheat the oil in a frying pan over medium heat. Dip the top part of the canapé in the egg, place one coriander leaf and red chili slice on top. Fry the canapés, top part facing down in the oil until golden. Remove from the pan with a strainer and drain excess oil. Ready to be served with the dipping sauce on the side.

Tips

Canapés made from wholesome bread will not absorb oil when deep-frying. This crispy bread can also be eaten with other dipping sauce such as tamarind peanut sauce.

Toong Tong

Deep-Fried Golden Pouches

The filling of these little pouches should be tasty. The pouches should be golden after deep-frying and not be oily. Golden pouches must be fried twice over different oil temperature. Pre-frying takes 2 minutes over medium heat, while second deep-frying takes 3 minutes over high heat until golden. This deep-frying method will keep the golden pouches from being too oily.

Filling

200g minced prawn meat
100g minced pork
50g yam bean or water chestnuts, cut into small cubes
15g fish sauce
½ ground sea salt
5 peppercorns
10g chopped coriander roots
15g garlic
30g vegetable oil
10g chopped garlic for frying

Other ingredients

30 small spring roll sheets, 5 in. diameter
4 stalks Chinese celery, split into strands, parboil in boiling water (used to tie the pouches)
1,000g palm oil for deep-frying

Finely pound the peppercorns, coriander roots, garlic, and salt together • Add the pounded mixture and other ingredients (except the oil and garlic for frying) into a mixing bowl and mix well • Preheat the oil in a frying pan. As the oil heats up, add the garlic and fry until fragrant. Add the meat mixture and stir-fry until cooked and dried. Set aside.

Make golden pouches

Place the spring roll sheets on a cutting board, smooth surface upwards. Spoon 25g of filling onto the center, form small pouches with the filling inside and tie the opening with the celery strings. Use scissors to trim the excess edges if necessary • Preheat the oil in a pan over medium heat. Deep-fry the golden pouches for 2 min. until they begin to cook (pre-frying must not fry the pouches until golden), then remove from the pan with a strainer and drain access oil. When the pouches are cool, store in a container by arranging the pouches in layers, separating each layer with grease paper. Cover and keep refrigerated.

For 1 serving of toong tong

6 golden pouches
4 bite-size pineapple
250g palm oil for deep-frying
30g spring roll dipping sauce

Preheat the oil in a pan over high heat. Deep-fry the golden pouches until golden. Remove from the pan with a strainer and drain access oil. Ready to be served with dipping sauce on the side, bite-size pineapple, or pickled ginger.

DESSERTS

Gluai Buad Chee (Banana in Coconut Milk)
Tubtim Grob (Tapioca Coated Water Chesnut in Syrup
   and Coconut Milk)
Bua Loi Sam See (Tri-Color Dumplings in Sweet
   Coconut Milk)
Bua Loi Sakoo (Tapioca in Sweet Coconut Milk)

Gluai Buad Chee

Banana in Coconut Milk

Bananas used in this dessert must be namwa variety. They should be tasted first. If the bananas are sweet, the sugar portion should be reduced. Each banana should be evenly cooked. The sweetness should be well-balanced, not too sweet and the coconut milk should not curdle.

Sweet coconut milk

125g thick coconut milk
750g thin coconut milk (375g thick
 coconut milk mixed with 375g water)
100g sugar
5g ground sea salt

Heat the thin coconut milk in a pot over medium heat. Add the sugar and salt and stir until sugar dissolves. Add the thick coconut milk and continue to cook for 1 min. Increase to high heat while stirring. Remove from the heat, leave to cool. Set aside in a closed container and keep refrigerated.

Other ingredients

10 ripe bananas (gluai namwa),
 with skins
30g yellow mung beans

Wash the bananas and add to boiling water to cook for 15-20 min. until cooked. Remove the bananas from the pot • Peel the cooked bananas and halve the banana vertically, then cut across in half (1 banana can be cut into 4 sections) • Wash the mung beans and soak in water for 30 min. Scoop out the beans and leave to drain excess water. Roast the beans in a pan over low heat until fragrant.

For **1** serving of gluai buad chee

1½ cooked banana (6 pieces)
140g sweet coconut milk
1 tsp roasted yellow mung beans

Heat the bananas and coconut milk over medium heat until the mixture is thoroughly warm. Serve in a bowl with roasted mung beans sprinkled on top.

Tips

Water should be boiling before adding the bananas. Cooking the bananas thoroughly will enhance the nature sweetness. Overcooked banana will be too soft, while undercooked banana will have bitter taste. Adding uncooked bananas to the coconut milk will cause the coconut milk to darken because it will coat the bananas and prevent the bananas from being cooked evenly. Lady Finger bananas (Gluai Khai) can also be used for this dish, using the same cooking process.

Tubtim Grob

Tapioca Coated Water Chestnut in Syrup and Coconut Milk

The coating flour in this dish should not be too soft, while the water chestnuts should be crispy. The coconut milk should not be overly sweet with some jasmine aroma.

Clear syrup
100g sugar
250g water

Heat the water and sugar over medium heat until the sugar dissolves. Set aside in a bowl. (The syrup is used to soak the coated water chestnuts.)

Syrup and coconut milk
200g sugar
140g jasmine scented water
250g thick coconut milk

Simmer the jasmine water and sugar over low heat until the syrup thickens. Set the syrup aside in a bowl • Bring the coconut milk to a boil in a pot. Set the coconut milk aside in a bowl.

Coated water chestnuts
300g raw water chestnuts or yam beans
200g tapioca flour
100g red syrup
5 cups of water

Cut the water chestnuts or yam beans in small cubes of ¼ inches. Soak the water chestnuts or yam beans in the red syrup until they absorb the red coloring • Scoop out the cubes and toss in tapioca flour ensuring thick coats of flour. Place on a strainer to shift off excess flour • Boil the coated water chestnuts in boiling water but adding small portions at a time. Cooked coated water chestnuts will float to the surface. Scoop out and immediately soak in cold water. As they are cool down, drain off excess water in a strainer. Soak the cooked stuffed water chestnuts in the clear syrup.

For 1 serving of tubtim grob
30g syrup
50g thick coconut milk
40g coated water chestnuts
4-5 small ice cubes

Mix the syrup and coconut milk together and heat the mixture until it is warm. Set aside in a bowl and leave the mixture to cool • Place the coated water chestnuts in a small bowl. Add the syrup and coconut milk and top with ice.

Tips
Avoid overcooking the coated water chestnuts because the flour will become soft. As the chestnuts rise to the surface of the boiling water, scoop out and soak in cold water immediately. Raw chestnuts or yam beans absorb red coloring better than the cooked ones. Soaking the coated water chestnuts in the syrup helps retain the shapes of the flour coating.
Using jasmine scented water to cook the syrup is preferred over plain water or smoke scented water. To make jasmine scented water: place 4 cups of water in a stainless steel pot with a lid. Float the jasmine buds (sepals removed) on the entire surface of the water, close the lid and leave the water overnight. Remove the jasmine buds from the water early in the morning. Leaving the jasmine buds too long will cause unpleasant scent.

Bua Loi Sam See

Tri-Color Dumplings in Sweet Coconut Milk

The dumplings should be soft and chewy. The coconut milk should not be overly sweet. The water should be boiling before adding the dumplings. Once the dumplings float up to the surface, allow the dumplings to float for about 30 seconds before scooping them out to soak in cold water.

Sweet coconut milk

880g thin coconut milk (440g thick
   coconut milk mixed with 440g water)
280g palm sugar
50g granulated sugar
5g ground sea salt

Mix the thin coconut milk with palm sugar, granulated sugar, and salt. Heat the mixture over medium heat until the sugar dissolves. Remove from the heat.

White dumplings

100g glutinous flour
60-120g water

Knead the flour with water by gradually adding the water bit by bit. Continue kneading until the mixture turns into a sticky soft dough. Roll the dough into a thing long logs, about the size of a pencil • Cut the dough into 1 cm pieces. Mold each piece into a small round shape, similar to the size of lotus seeds • Cook the dough in boiling water. The cooked dumplings will float up to the surface. Scoop the dumplings out and immediately soak in cold water. As the dumplings cool down, add some sweet coconut milk to prevent the dumplings from sticking.

Taro dumplings

50g glutinous flour
100g steamed and mashed taro
30-50g water

Mix the glutinous flour and mashed taro together. Knead the mixture as gradually adding the water bit by bit until it turns into a sticky soft dough. Mold the dough and cook the dumplings with the same method.

Pumpkin dumplings

50g glutinous flour
60g steamed and mashed pumpkin

Mix the glutinous flour and mashed pumpkin together. Knead the mixture until it turns into a sticky soft dough. Sprinkle some water if the mixture is dry. Mold the dough and cook the dumplings with the same method.

For **1** serving of bua loi sam see

120g sweet coconut milk
60-75g tri-color dumplings
   (25g for each color)

Heat the sweet coconut milk in a pot over medium heat until warm. Add the dumplings. Ready to be served in a dessert bowl.

Tips

Pre-boiling the dumplings will retain the shapes, as well as the soft and chewy texture of the dumplings. Cooking the dumplings in the sweet coconut milk will cause the dumplings to become too soft and soggy because the flour will be overcooked. The dumplings will become sticky. Pumpkin dumplings does not require water because pumpkin is very moist.

Bua Loi Sakoo

Tapioca in Sweet Coconut Milk

The tapioca pearls in this dish should be cooked and soft but not mushy. The sweet coconut milk not be too thick and it should have well-balanced flavors with sweet aroma from the sugar.

Sweet coconut milk
250g palm sugar
1,000g thin coconut milk (625g thick coconut mixed with 375g water)
5g ground sea salt

Mix the thincoconut milk, sugar, and salt in a pot. Stir the mixture together before placing over medium heat. Bring the mixture to a boil, then remove from the heat.

Other ingredients
200g grated young coconut (thin long strands)
125g boiled corns (slice off the corns from the cobs)
250g large tapioca

Toss the tapioca pearls to remove the flour dust. Boil 8 cups of water in a pot, add the tapioca and boil for 20 min. (frequently while boiling to prevent the tapioca from stick-ing) • Remove the pot from the heat and leave the tapioca in the pot for 1 hour before draining off the water • Boil 5 cups of water in a pot. Add the tapioca and boil until the tapioca begin to cook thoroughly (visible white dots in the middle). Scoop out and soak the tapioca in clear syrup (refer to Stuffed Water Chestnut in Coconut Milk recipe).

For 1 serving of bua loi sakoo
50g tapioca pearls
20g grated young coconut
20g boiled corns
120g sweet coconut milk

Heat the sweet coconut milk in a pot over medium heat until warm. Add the tapioca, grated coconut, and corn. Stir well until thoroughly warm. Ready to be served in a dessert bowl.

Tips
Cooked tapioca should be soaked in clear syrup rather than plain water in order to retain the texture. Leaving the tapioca too long in sweet coconut milk can cause the milk to thicken, therefore the dessert should be prepared just before serving.

INGREDIENTS AND CURRY PASTES

THAI HERBS:
GOODNESS REVEALED

One of the reasons for the popularity of Thai food is the use of many kinds of spices and herbs. The tropical climate of Thailand favors the growth of variety of fragrant plants, which are used freely in Thai dishes. Almost every part of these plants can be used, i.e. leaves, stems, fruits, and even roots. There are different ways to use the spices and herbs, either singly or in combination. Each combination results in a different aroma distinctive of different dish. *Choo chee* curry carries the fragrance of the rind of bitter orange while *panang* curry has the aroma of roasted coriander seeds. Besides giving a pleasant aroma, spices and herbs enhance the flavor and cover the sour smell of meat, poultry and fish. Fresh herbs also add both nutritional and medicinal value to Thai dishes. Lemongrass in *tom yum goong* (clear prawn soup) improves the shrimp flavor, gives a well balanced taste to the soup when the lemongrass stick is chewed on, and has healing purposes, such as aiding digestion and supplementing fiber, iron, and the B-vitamins.

Basic ingredients of the herb mixture in Thai cooking are chili, garlic, and shallot. These are pounded together to form a paste. Additional herbs and/or spices make different kinds of preparations. The paste can be dissolved in water or cooked in oil/coconut milk before adding meat and vegetables. Fresh herbs are always added last for a better flavor and appearance.

Herbs must be used in the right amount to give a pleasant flavor. Adding too little is not enough, while adding too much makes the dish smell like medicine. To make Thai red or green curry paste, 5 dried chilies or 20 fresh small hot chilies (known as bird's eye chilies or Thai chilies) require 3 tsp of shallot, 1 tsp of chopped coriander roots, 5 peppercorns, 1 tbsp of roasted coriander seeds, ½ tsp of bitter orange rind, 1 tsp of roasted cumin, 1 tsp of chopped galangal, and 1 tsp of chopped lemongrass. Extra amount of any herbs will destroy the well-blended flavor of the curry.

The following are some of the more frequently used herbs and their medicinal properties:

Garlic *(gra-tium)* Garlic is ground into curry paste, crushed in salad dressings or chopped up and fried before adding other ingredients in stir-fry dishes. Garlic cures and prevents atherosclerosis and high blood pressure, aids digestion, relieves cold symptoms, and fights some intestinal parasites.

Shallot *(hua hom)* Shallot is pounded into curry pastes or sauces, or cut up finely in salads and stir-fry dishes. This herb is diuretic, helps digestion, increases appetite, releases gas and phlegm, and helps fight colds.

Holy basil *(ga-prao)* Add fresh holy basil leaves to the stir-fried ingredients just before removing from heat. The heated basil will add flavor to the preparation and crisply fried holy basil can be used as garnish for *pad gaprao* dishes. Holy basil is known to relieve flatulence, help release gas, release phlegm, and increase lactation.

Sweet basil *(horapa)* Added to the cooked dishes just before removing from the heat, sweet basil gives off the most fragrance when heated but not overcooked. Sweet basil aids digestion, increases perspiration, relieves coughing, fights parasites of the digestive tract, relieves constipation, and cures scurvy.

Hoary basil leaves *(bai maeng luk)* This herb, which is also called hairy basil and lemon basil, is best while fresh. It is the last ingredient to be added to spicy vegetable soup just before removal from heat. It aids digestion, increases perspiration, relieves coughing, and cures scurvy.

Kaffir lime leaves *(bai ma-grood)* Whole leaves are used in *tom yum*, *tom kha*, red or green curry, *gaeng kua*, *panang*, *choo chee*, and spicy fried fish, chicken or pork. Finely shredded leaves are used in salads. Kaffir lime leaves help relieve cramps and release gas.

Ginger root *(khing)* Shredded ginger is an essential ingredient in *tom som pla-tu* (mackerel in tamarind soup). The cooked ginger will give off its flavor, softening the hot taste. Ginger root aids digestion, helps release phlegm, relieves stomachache and nausea, increases perspiration, and dilates capillaries.

Fingerroot *(gra-chai)* Used in *hor mok pla chon* (steamed fish with curry paste in banana leaf cup), fingerroot stops diarrhea, relieves stomach ache, flatulence, cough, and is good for the heart.

Turmeric *(kha-min)* Used in many Thai curry pastes, this herb releases gas, helps relieve stomach ache, and muscle stress, promotes plasma flow, and helps regulate menstruation.

Lemongrass *(ta-krai)* Lemongrass is an essential ingredient of *tom yum*, a popular dish served in most Thai restaurants around the world. This herb gives a pleasant flavor and covers the fish and shrimp smell. Lemongrass aids digestion, relieves stomach pain, increases urine production, relieves gall stone problems, and relieves high blood pressure.

Young galangal root *(kha on)* An essential ingredient of a delicious and popular dish, chicken in coconut mlk soup or *tom kha gai*, galangal gives a pleasant flavor, covers up the natural chicken smell and nullifies the fatty taste of the coconut milk. Young galangal relieves skin rashes, diarrhea, indigestion, and bodily pains.

Mature galangal *(kha gae)* Beef and chicken *tom yum* need mature galangal root to improve the flavor of the beef and chicken. The dishes will have a better aroma and taste with this herb. Mature galangal relieves rashes, stops diarrhea, releases gas, relieves flatulence, helps digestion, and relieves swelling and bruises.

Pepper *(prik Thai)* Used in *gaeng liang* and red curry paste. Ground pepper is sprinkled on stir-fried dishes, stir-fried meat, soups and rice congee or Asian rice porridge. Pepper helps digestion, releases gas, improves food flavor, covers undesirable meat and fish smell, and helps protect eye tissue.

Lime *(Ma-now)* Used in salad dressing and *tom yum*, lime helps relieve cough and sore throat, dissolve phlegm, cure swollen gums and scurvy, cure vitamin C deficiency diseases, and relieve dizziness and constipation.

Mint *(Saranae)* Used in most spicy salads, this herb helps release gas, disinfect, and relieve stomach and intestine muscle rigidity.

HERBS AND SPICES
IN THAI COOKING

Herbs and spices play a very important role in their contribution to making Thai food delicious. Thai cooks must know the qualities of herbs and spices, as well as the selection method for the correct and proper amount of herbs and spices for any particular dish.

Herbs (fresh ingredients) include shallot, garlic, ginger, galangal, lemongrass, kafir lime zest, coriander root, turmeric, chilies, and etc. These also include fresh leaves such as sweet basil, holy basil, mint, hoary basil, coriander, kaffir lime leaves, and etc. Look for freshness, and do not store for long periods of time.

Spices (dried ingredients) include dried seeds, flowers, bark, roots, and leaves, which all possess different aromas and tastes. Therefore, the amount of spices used is not much. Look for freshness and strength of aroma when selecting spices. Spices should be bought only as much as needed. Coriander seed, cumin and pepper should be bought whole; they need to be freshly roasted and ground to give better aroma.

SELECTION AND STORAGE
OF HERBS AND SPICES

Garden grown small, hot chili (bird's eye chili, *prik kee noo)* Store them directly without washing. Wrap the chili in paper and refrigerate; this way, they can be stored for a long time without rotting or wilting. Take the stems out and wash before use.

Large dried chili *(prik haeng)* Select completely dried pods, dark red in color. The pods should be long and whole with stems attached. They must not be broken or moldy, with no musty smell. They should be kept in a bamboo container or bamboo basket.

Medium green, yellow, and red spur chili *(prik chee fa)* Select round pods of equal size, beautiful and even in color without blemishes. The stems should be fresh.

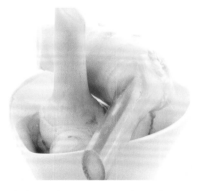

Thai garlic Select large sections with firm flesh, fully mature and not soft. (Young garlic will become soft easily.) Store the garlic in the same way as dried chilies, in a low humidity environment, so that they will not become moldy. Thai garlic has a stronger aroma than garlic grown in other countries. If the latter is used in *nam prik gapi,* the garlic will not be able to cover or reduce the shrimp paste smell as well as Thai garlic.

Shallot Select large heads, dry and not soft. Thai shallot has better aroma and taste than that grown in other countries (Indian shallot). Usually there is black mold on the shallot. Soak in water before peeling, and then wash again afterwards. Fried Thai shallot is crispier than Indian shallot because the latter has more starch content. If Thai garlic and shallot are not used in curry pastes, the curry pastes will be pasty as if starch was added.

Galangal Mature galangal root gives better aroma to curry pastes. Select brown skinned mature roots with fresh and not wilted joints. In *tom kha gai* (chicken in coconut milk soup), young galangal root is used. Crushed mature galangal root is used in boiling coconut milk soup to give a nice aroma to the soup. Young galangal root is pearly white with pink tips.

Fingerroot or Chinese ginger Select large round fresh roots. Store them in water in the same way that lemongrass is stored. Soak in water for a while before use. The skin will then be scraped off, washed, and cut according to the directions shown in the recipe.

Kaffir lime Select mature, large, and fresh fruit. The skin should not be smooth. Deep green fruits have a stronger aroma than the soft green ones.

Lime Select green fruit with thin rind. The outer part of the fruit must be smooth. Thai *Paen* lime gives more juice with thin rind and is not bitter.

Lemongrass Select big, round, fresh stalks. Make sure the outer leaves are not dried or wilted. Cut ½ inch off the bottom part before use. Lemongrass and galangal can be kept for 4 to 5 days by immersing the largest part in clean water. Sometimes the roots will grow when the herbs are placed in a deep dish of water (e.g. a vase).

Coriander seed They are small, round, pale brown aromatic seeds. Coriander seed should be roasted, ground and used immediately.

Cumin They are small, oblong, pale brown seeds. Cumin gives off a stronger smell than coriander seeds. They should be roasted and ground just before use.

Nutmeg These are large, oblong, dark brown seeds with hard outer parts. The hard outer part is cracked off before use. Only the inner brown aromatic flesh is used. They are cracked into small pieces, roasted and ground immediately before use.

Nutmeg petals They are the long and thin brown petals of the nutmeg, which are easily brken. Nutmeg petals should be roasted and ground immediately before use.

Cloves They are dark brown sticks with knots on the top resembling nails. These knots are flower buds. Cloves have a strong smell and a hot taste. Cloves need to be roasted and ground before use.

Cardamom They are small, white, and round fruits with skin that can be easily peeled off. The seed inside is black, aromatic, and a little hot. When using in *massaman* curry, use the whole fruit. The outer skin needs not be peeled off. Cardamoms are roasted before being used whole in the curry.

Cinnamon It is the hard bark of a tree. When it dries, the bark will roll into a stick. When it is used in curry paste, it must be heated in a dry skillet or roasted first to be aromatic.

Pepper The white, round seeds are mature pepper. They are called "prik Thai lon" in Thai. The black pepper is immature and has skin covering the seeds. The white pepper is preferred as it is aromatic and hot. When not available, black pepper can be used.

Curry powder This is a yellow and aromatic mixture of ground spices, such as turmeric, coriander seeds, cumin, ginger, cloves, cinnamon, and dried chilies. They are popularly used in curry and many other dishes. Choose the kind that has been recently packed in bottles. When purchasing from stores that only

carry spices in bulks, select the store which sells spices exclusively. The curry powder sold in regular grocery stores may not be of high quality. Keep in mind that curry powder will not have a strong scent when stored for too long.

FRESH VEGETABLES

Buy fresh, recently cut vegetables for immediate use. Cooks need to know the characteristics of each kind of vegetable used with each dish.

Cucumber Choose the dark green fruits. There should be 20 cucumbers per kilogram. The number per kilogram is important as the cucumbers will be of the same size. The pearly white cucumbers have more seeds than flesh.

Long cucumber (*taeng ran*) The fruit is green, long, and straight. Select the fruit which is about 150 grams in weight.

Cockroach berry (*ma-kuea proh*) Select dull green fruits. The shiny ones are too mature with hard seeds. There should be 25-30 fruits per kilogram.

Onion Select the ones with brown skin. Choose ones that are equal in size about 100 grams each.

Potato Select long straight dark brown ones which are equal in size with each weighing about 200 grams. Selecting equally sized fruits will make the preparation process easier. For example, you can cut one potato into 8 equal pieces of 25 grams.

Green bean and string bean Select straight firm ones that are of green color evenly along the bean. The bean should not be swollen or broken. Buy only enough for not more than two days use.

Sweet pea Buy the evenly green peas. They should not be swollen or shiny. Buy only enough for not more than two days use.

Pineapple Select green fruit for dishes used at meals. The yellow ones are ripened and not good for cooking, as sometimes they do not smell good and are not sour enough.

Tomato Use cherry tomatoes (about 10 grams each) in soup or curry. Large tomatoes (about 100 grams each) with thick flesh are used for pan-frying, for instance, sweet and sour dishes.

CONDIMENTS IN THAI FOOD

Shrimp paste Select fine texture paste that smells good. The shrimp paste must be at the right consistency, not too soft or too dry. Low quality shrimp paste has yellowish powder on the top.

Fish sauce Select clear, reddish brown fish sauce. There should be no sediment at the bottom of the container. The Food and Drug Administration of Thailand requires 20 percent sodium content. The more sodium it contains, the saltier the fish sauce will be.

Sugar Avoid the very white sugar because it has been chemically bleached. Use the kind of sugar specified in the recipe to make a delicious dish. (Do not use brown sugar in cooking.)

Palm sugar (coconut sugar) The soft kind is better than the hard kind. Choose the light brown colored type because that is the natural color of the sugar. Do not use chemically bleached sugar. Pearly white sugar is less aromatic than light brown sugar.

Tamarind Select light brown tamarind fruit as the dark brown ones have been stored for a long time. Tamarinds must be squeezed immediately. Use two kilograms of water with one kilogram of tamarind fruits. The water is separated into three parts and the tamarind

is squeezed three times. Put the tamarind liquid through a strainer, then boil and refrigerate. This can be kept for three to four months. If it is not boiled, it will be spoilt – spoilt liquid tamarind smells bad and turns dark brown in color.

CURRY PASTES

Exotic Thai curry paste comes in vast varieties. Each region has its own unique recipe for curry paste. The essential ingredients are chili, onion, garlic, galangal, and lemongrass. Coriander seed, cumin, kaffir lime, fingerroot, sweet basil, holy basil, etc, are also added to certain types of curry pastes to bring out distinctive spicy flavors. The mixture is pulverized and formed into paste for use in cooking. Curry paste can significantly enhance spicy fragrances and tantalize taste buds to flavors of fried food and curry dishes.

Ready-made paste is called curry paste or chili paste. The paste must be smooth in texture for it to blend well with soup. Improperly pounded paste contains heavy items such as pieces of chili that will settle at the bottom of the curry soup, making the broth more watery than it should be. By cutting the ingredients into smaller pieces, the pounding is much easier and faster. Remove the seeds from the dried chili first. Then, soak in water before squeezing the water out. Cut into fine pieces and pound with mortar and pestle. Salt can be added to make pounding easier. Tougher ingredients such as galangal, lemongrass, kaffir lime rind, and coriander root should be added next. When they are well pounded, onion and garlic, which are more watery, can be added. Other spices such as coriander seeds, cumin, clove, and nutmeg should be lightly pan-toasted before being pounded with the mixture to acquire aromatic flavors and delightful fragrances.

The ready-made curry paste must be precooked before storing or cooking. Usually, this is done by frying in oil. To make 1 kilogram of green curry paste or holy basil curry paste, fry the curry paste with ¼ cup of vegetable oil for about 5 minutes. Do not overheat or burn. Coconut milk can be added bit by bit at a time – the amount depends on each recipe. Precooked curry paste retains its natural color, aroma and flavors even when it is kept in refrigeration for quite a while. Without precooking, certain enzymes can cause the curry paste to turn stale.

Curry paste can be used in cooking a variety of dishes: stir-fried dishes such as stir-fried chicke with holy basil; dishes sautéed in coconut milk with a small amount of liquid such as panang curry; grilled and steamed food such as steamed fish curry and northern Thai sausages; clear curry soups such as tamarind curry and yellow curry; coconut milk curry soups such as red curry and massaman curry, and more.

Dishes containing coconut milk can go off quite easily, especially in the summer. While cooking, the chef should thoroughly boil the soup. After cooked, curry dishes should not be tightly covered while still hot.

Green Curry Paste

20 green bird's eye chilies
5 medium green spur chilies, finely sliced
1 tsp ground sea salt
1 tsp finely cut galangal
1 tbsp finely cut lemongrass
½ tsp finely cut kaffir lime rind
1 tsp finely cut coriander root
5 peppercorns
4 tbsp sliced shallots
2 tbsp sliced garlic
1 tbsp ground roasted coriander seeds
1 tsp ground roasted cumin
1 tsp shrimp paste

Pound together the two kinds of green chilies and salt. Add galangal, lemongrass, kaffir lime rind, coriander root and peppercorns. Pound together finely. Add shallot, garlic and the rest of the ingredients. Pound until well mixed. Add shrimp paste and pound until smooth. (Yield about 120 grams of curry paste.) • Put 2 tbsp of vegetable oil into a skillet. Place over low heat. Fry the curry paste for about 3 minutes when the oil is warm. Transfer the mixture into a container.

Choo Chee Curry Paste

5 deseeded large dried chilies, soaked till softened
1 tsp ground sea salt
1 tsp finely cut galangal
1 tbsp finely cut lemongrass
½ tsp finely cut kaffir lime rind
1 tsp finely cut coriander roots
5 tbsp sliced shallots
2 tbsp sliced garlic
1 tsp shrimp paste

Squeeze-dry the soaked dried chilies and cut finely. Pound the dried chilies with salt. Add galangal, lemongrass, kaffir lime rind and coriander root. Pound together finely. Add shallots, garlic and pound until well mixed. Add the shrimp paste and pound together finely. (Yield about 100 grams of curry paste.) • Put 2 tbsp of vegetable oil into a skillet and place over low heat. When the oil is warm, fry the curry mixture for about 3 minutes. Transfer into a container.

Red Curry Paste

5 deseeded large dried chilies, soaked till softened
1 tsp ground sea salt
2 tsp finely cut galangal
1 tbsp roasted coriander seeds
1 tsp roasted finely cut *proh* (aromatic ginger or sand ginger, used only in red curry paste for roasted duck red curry)
2 tsp finely cut coriander roots
1 tsp finely cut kaffir lime rind
1 tbsp finely cut lemongrass
1 tsp ground roasted nutmeg (used only in red curry paste for roasted duck red curry)
2 tsp ground roasted cumin
5 peppercorns
3 tbsp sliced shallots
2 tbsp sliced garlic
1 tbsp shrimp paste

Squeeze-dry the soaked chilies and cut finely. Finely pound the chilies with salt. Add the remaining ingredients except shallots, garlic and shrimp paste. Pound until well mixed. Add shallot and garlic. Pound together and add shrimp paste. Pound until smooth. (Yield about 120 grams of curry paste.) • Put 2 tbsp of vegetable oil into a skillet. Place over low heat. Fry the curry paste about 3 minutes when the oil is warm. Transfer into a container.

Panang Curry Paste

6-7 deseeded large dried chilies, soaked till softened
1 tsp ground sea salt
1 tsp finely cut galangal
1 tbsp finely cut lemongrass
½ tbsp finely cut coriander root
½ tbsp finely cut kaffir lime rind
5 peppercorns
4 tbsp sliced shallots
2 tbsp sliced garlic
1 tbsp ground roasted coriander seeds
½ tsp ground roasted cumin
1 tsp shrimp paste

Squeeze-dry the soaked chilies and cut finely. Finely pound the chilies with salt. Add galangal, lemongrass, coriander roots, kaffir lime rind and peppercorns. Pound until well mixed. Add shallots and garlic and pound together. Add the remaining spices and pound until well mixed. Add the shrimp paste and pound until smooth. (Yield about 120 grams of curry paste.) • Put 2 tbsp of vegetable oil into a skillet. Place over low heat. Fry the curry paste about 3 minutes when the oil is warm. Transfer into a container.

Chili Curry Paste

5 deseeded large dried chilies, soaked till softened
1 tsp ground sea salt
1 tsp finely cut galangal
1 tbsp finely cut lemongrass
4 tbsp sliced shallots
2 tbsp sliced garlic
1 tsp shrimp paste

Squeeze dry the soaked chilies, and cut finely. Finely pound the chilies with salt. Add galangal and lemongrass. Pound until very fine. Add shallots and garlic and pound until well mixed. Add shrimp paste and pound until smooth. (Yield about 100 grams of curry paste.) • Put 2 tbsp of vegetable oil into a skillet. Place over low heat. Fry the curry paste about 3 minutes when the oil is warm. Transfer into a container.

Pad Prik Khing Curry Paste

5 deseeded large dried chilies, soaked till softened
1 tsp ground sea salt
1 tsp finely cut galangal
1 tbsp finely cut lemongrass
1 tsp finely cut kaffir lime rind
1 tsp finely cut coriander roots
5 peppercorns
5 tbsp sliced shallots
2 tbsp sliced garlic
1 tsp shrimp paste
3 tbsp ground dried shrimps

Squeeze dry the soaked dried chilies and cut finely. Finely pound the chilies and salt together. Add galangal, lemongrass, kaffir lime rind, coriander roots and peppercorns until very fine. Add shallots and garlic and pound again. Add shrimp paste and dried shrimps. Pound until smooth. (Yield about 120 grams curry paste.) • Put 2 tbsp of vegetable oil into a skillet. Place over low heat. Fry the curry paste about 3 minutes when the oil is warm. Transfer into a container.

Massaman Cury Paste

3 deseeded large dried chilies, soaked till softened
1 tsp ground sea salt
3 slices of roasted galangal
2 tbsp roasted finely cut lemongrass
1 tbsp roasted finely cut coriander roots
3 tbsp roasted sliced shallots
1 tbsp roasted coriander seeds
12 cloves of roasted peeled garlic
12 peppercorns
1 tsp roasted cumin
½ tsp roasted nutmeg flesh
2 roasted cardamom seeds
1 ½ cm-long roasted cinnamon stick
2 cloves
1tsp grilled shrimp paste

Finely pound the dried chilies, salt, galangal, lemongrass, coriander roots and peppercorns together. Add shallots and garlic and pound together. Add the remaining spices and pound till well mixed. Add the shrimp paste and pound until smooth. (Yield about 120 grams of curry paste.)
• Put 2 tbsp of vegetable oil in a skillet. Place over low heat. Fry the curry paste about 3 minutes when the oil is warm. Transfer into a container.

Yellow Curry Paste

3 deseeded large dried chilies, soaked till softened
1 tsp ground sea salt
1 tsp finely cut galangal
1 tbsp finely cut lemongrass
1 tsp roasted finely cut ginger
5 tbsp grilled or roasted shallots
2 tbsp grilled or roasted garlic
1 tbsp ground roasted coriander seeds
1 tsp ground roasted cumin
2 tsp curry powder
1 tsp shrimp paste

Squeeze-dry the soaked chilies and cut finely. Finely pound the chilies and salt together, Add galangal, lemongrass and ginger and pound finely. Add shallot and garlic. Pound till well mixed. Add the remaining spices. Pound until mixed together. Add the shrimp paste and pound until smooth. (Yield about 120 grams curry paste.)
• Put 2 tbsp of vegetable oil into a skillet. Place over low heat. When the oil is warm, fry the curry paste about 3 minutes. Transfer into a container.

Holy Basil Curry Paste

10 finely cut yellow spur chilies
10 finely cut red spur chilies
1 tsp ground sea salt
1 tbsp finely cut galangal
1 tbsp finely cut coriander roots
6 tbsp sliced garlic

Finely pound the chilies together with salt. Add galangal and coriander roots and pound together. Add garlic and pound until well mixed. (Yield about 100 grams of the herb mixture.) • Put 2 tbsp of vegetable oil into a skillet. Place over low heat. Fry the curry paste about 3 minutes when the oil is warm. Transfer into a container.

HOW TO MAKE YOUR THAI FOOD ATTRACTIVE

Factors in making your Thai dishes attractive and inviting are:

- Care in cutting and slicing, making pieces equal and uniform.
- Contrasting shapes and colors of food arranged in one dish is also important.
- Correct characteristics. For example, crispy food must be crisp when served.
- Specific aroma and taste of each dish. For example, *choo chee* must have the aroma of kaffir lime zest and the sweetness of coconut milk. *Panang* should have the aroma of coriander seeds in the curry paste to make it stronger and hotter in taste than *choo chee*.
- Proper use of container. For example, *choo chee*, which has a lot of liquid, should be served in a deep dish but not in a bowl. *Panang* has less liquid and should be served in a shallow dish to make it look delicious.
- Edible garnish should be used. *Choo chee* with shredded kaffir lime leaf sprinkled on top is better than that topped with rich coconut milk. Green curry needs not be served with fresh sweet basil leaves on top because the basil will be wilted and will not look good. Red spur chili and sweet basil in the curry should be placed on top of the curry as it will look more inviting.
- Garnished vegetables and side-dish vegetables should be fresh and dry without a drop of water. Some dishes look better with proper garnish, such as bite-size pineapples placed along the *tod mun* (deep-fried shrimp/fish patties). Easily wilting vegetables should not be used.

SOME FINAL WORDS:
Just like to Let You Know

In writing cookbooks, one must pay attention to details. It must be written for people of different educational backgrounds to understand, not to be understood only by the author. Every recipe has to be actually made and tasted before writing. Readers cannot ask when they do not understand because each one has a different level of basic knowledge in cooking. All ingredients must be tasted. Despite the fact that some ingredients in a curry mixture may be used in a very small amount, such as a spice, it has to be included - for example, half a teaspoon of ground roasted coriander seeds. A spice must be roasted before being ground. It must be roasted, if not, it will not be aromatic. The readers must understand and be aware of the importance of herbs and spices, because if too much is used, the dish will smell like medicine. For every dish, preparation, cutting and slicing is different. For example, for *pad gaprao*, (stir-fried chicken with holy basil), ground tough meat is used; but for *pad kee-mao* (hot and spicy stir-fried dish), sliced tender meat is used. Therefore, it must be stated what part of meat is used. Two things that are essential in a recipe are the characteristics and tastes of the dish which act as a guideline for evaluation of the finished dish.

Many cooks, especially foreigners, do not understand the method of Thai food preparation. For example, in *pad gaprao*, the ground chicken or pork need to be cooked first. Chicken in the green curry must be cooked in coconut milk first. Papaya in papaya salad must be pounded till soft before the sauce is added. Curry pastes for almost all curries, except only **gaeng som** (sour curry) must first be fried in coconut milk or oil. If the curry paste is not fried first, the curry will not have the characteristic aroma. The taste will be off. Fish sauce in a soup must be added after the soup is boiling for the soup to be aromatic and not smell fishy. Fish must be added after the stock is boiling to eliminate the fishy smell. The curry pastes for *gaeng som* must be added to boiling water to bring the aroma into the liquid.

Foreigners tend to think that all Thai dishes contain curry mixture and coconut milk and taste hot, when actually, not all Thai dishes taste hot. Depending on what dish it is, for instance, *choo chee* is sweeter than *panang*, and green curry is hotter than red curry. Foreigners also may think all Thai dishes are hot, and that fried dishes are not Thai food. But actually, we have fried, deep-fried, grilled, roasted, steamed, boiled, and many more.

There are many things misunderstood by most people. For example only eggplants should be added to red or green curries. Galangal and chili sauce are not used in *tom yum goong*. Many things make Thai cooking something for each cook to decide. The reason for putting vegetables into the curry is to make one compliment the other. Pea eggplants in green curries help tone down the heat and the oily taste of the liquid. They equalize and harmonize the tastes.

Thai food is attractive. It contains several tastes that complement each other nicely. It gives a nice feeling to the act of eating. It has medicinal and nutritional value. I would like to share our good things with people all around the world. I would like people to be able to cook Thai food, and there is no other way to do this than to write cookbooks, using simple language most people can read and understand, hoping to promote the use of Thai herbs and spices. There is also a need to improve the growing of Thai herbs and spices along with the promotion of Thai food. We need to grow holy basil and sweet basil that can be kept longer and are more resistant to diseases.

I have always wanted to have a modern, cool, and clean kitchen like a Western kitchen. Now I have one where anyone can come to learn to cook. I have also long wanted a flexible course for everyone to meet their needs. Now with my own cooking school, that can be done.

My other dream, which is only some percent fulfilled, is to be able to teach Thai cooking to foreigners. I have always thought that we Thais have to go abroad to learn international cooking; likewise, foreigners should come to learn Thai cooking in Thailand. Now that dream has come true.

Srisamorn Kongpun